Kenmore Microwave Cooking

D1279491

BENJAMIN

Home Economics Director: Virginia Peterson
Senior Home Economists: Thelma Pressman, Betty Sullivan,
    LuAnne Dugan
Managing Editor: Virginia Schomp
Editor: Naomi Galbreath
Editorial Assistants: Laurie Neinfeldt, Glen Gilchrist
Food Stylists: Carol Peterson, Jean Carey
Art & Design: Thomas C. Brecklin
Graphic Artist: Barbara Schwoegler
Typography: A-Line, Milwaukee
Photography: Teri Sandison, Los Angeles

USER INSTRUCTIONS
PRECAUTIONS TO AVOID POSSIBLE EXPOSURE TO EXCESSIVE MICRO-WAVE ENERGY

(a) DO NOT ATTEMPT to operate this oven with the door open since open-door operation can result in harmful exposure to microwave energy. It is important not to defeat or tamper with the safety interlocks.

(b) DO NOT PLACE any object between the oven front face and the door or allow soil or cleaner residue to accumulate on sealing surfaces.

(c) DO NOT OPERATE the oven if it is damaged. It is particularly important that the oven door close properly and that there is no damage to the:
> (1) DOOR (bent)
> (2) HINGES AND LATCHES (broken or loosened)
> (3) DOOR SEALS AND SEALING SURFACES

(d) THE OVEN SHOULD NOT BE ADJUSTED OR REPAIRED BY ANYONE EXCEPT PROPERLY QUALIFIED SERVICE PERSONNEL.

Library of Congress Catalog Card Number: 85-070585
ISBN: 0-87502-155-7
Published by the Benjamin Company, Inc.
One Westchester Plaza
Elmsford, New York 10523
Printed in Japan
10 9 8 7 6 5 4 3 2 — 13332

Table of Contents

HOW DOES IT WORK?

Congratulations! You have selected a superior cooking method, joining the countless thousands who have discovered the joys of the microwave oven and are delighted by this fast, easy, and efficient method of cooking. But, as with any new appliance, before you start to cook, you should take time to read the instructions carefully. These illustrated introductory chapters are designed to be a cooking school in book form. We will show and tell you all about the way the oven works, why it works that way, what it can do, and how to quickly become an accomplished microwave cook.

There is nothing complicated about using the oven; all you need is a little understanding of the special qualities of microwave cooking and you'll be on your way. Like any comprehensive conventional cookbook, this book tries to leave nothing to chance. We think you'll soon agree that cooking in the microwave oven is as easy as it looks. Take a few minutes to familiarize yourself with the principles and techniques of the oven — then try the wonderful recipes that begin on page 35.

To install your oven, follow the Use and Care manual's directions. The microwave oven requires little maintenance. Unlike a conventional oven, which generates heat in the oven cavity, there is no heat in the microwave cavity, so food and grease do not bake on. Just a simple wiping is all it occasionally needs.

The Principles

In conventional cooking by gas or electricity, food on top of the stove cooks by heat applied to the bottom of the pan, and in the oven by hot air, which surrounds the food. In microwave cooking, microwaves travel directly to the food, without heating the oven. Inside the microwave oven is a magnetron vacuum tube that converts ordinary electrical energy into high-frequency microwaves, just like radio and television waves. A fan-like device, called a stirrer, helps distribute the microwaves evenly throughout the oven. Microwaves are waves of energy, not heat. They are either reflected, passed through, or absorbed, depending upon the material contacted. For example, metal reflects microwaves; glass, pottery, paper, and most plastics allow the waves to pass through; and, finally, food absorbs microwaves. Very simply then, the absorbed microwave energy causes the food molecules to vibrate rapidly against each other, inducing friction, which in turn produces the heat that cooks the food. This is somewhat like the way heat is generated when you rub your hands together. The waves penetrate the food, and cooking begins from the exterior. The interior then cooks by conduction.

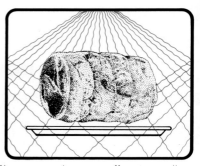

Microwaves bounce off oven walls and are absorbed by food. The air in the oven remains cool.

This process produces the much-appreciated cooking speed of the microwave oven. Because the cooking containers used in the microwave oven do not absorb microwave energy, they do not become hot. The microwaves pass through the containers directly into the food. However, the containers may absorb heat from the food itself, so you will occasionally need to use potholders. The see-through panel in the microwave oven door is made of a specially prepared material that contains a metal screen. The metal screen reflects the microwaves, yet enables you to observe the food as it cooks. The waves cannot penetrate this screen. Opening the microwave oven door turns the unit off automatically, so you can stir, turn, or check doneness with ease. And you don't have to face that blast of hot air you expect when opening a conventional oven.

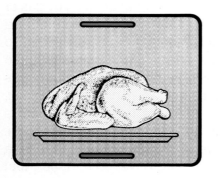

Conventional oven cooks by hot air.

WHAT IT DOES BEST

You can cook just about anything in the microwave oven, but some food is so especially good done this way that we want to show several of them to you. Let's take a look.

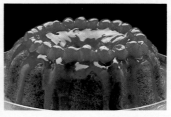

□ *Roast beef* is juicy and rare, with less shrinkage than in the conventional oven. □ *Vegetables* are at their best. Flavor and color are preserved and potatoes are fluffy. □ You'll want *scrambled eggs and bacon* for breakfast, lunch, and supper! Eggs are fluffier than in conventional cooking, and bacon cooks without turning or mess. □ *Cakes* are moist, rich and super-high. □ *Casseroles* cook without sticking and reheat with no trouble at all.

□ *Candy and bar cookies* are particular favorites for microwave cooks because they are easy as pie. Try this Peanut Brittle or the zesty Lemon Bars and see for yourself. □ The microwave can't be beaten for *reheating leftover platters, rolls, and bread* so quickly they are truly perfect.

□ Explore the pleasures of cooking *seafood* in your microwave oven. Fish fillets and steaks are moist and tender, their natural juices enhancing their delicate flavor. □ There's no equal to a *bowl of soup* or a cup of coffee served directly from the oven. □ *Melt butter (or chocolate)* in seconds and save the mess of burned pans or double boilers.

Now let's look at what you need to know to start cooking.

COOKING TECHNIQUES AND COOKWARE

In this chapter you will find everything you need to know to make microwave cooking easy, efficient, and pleasurable. Once you know the principles, the techniques will become second nature. Read this basic information with its accompanying illustrations carefully. Here you will learn why some foods cook faster than others, what you should know about timing and temperature, which cooking utensils and sizes are appropriate, and much more.

Because of the unique qualities of microwave energy, microwave cooking uses certain terms and methods that are different from those of conventional cooking. For example, in microwave cooking, many foods complete their cooking during standing time, either in the oven or after being removed from the oven. In addition, how food is arranged in the cooking dish is important to its being cooked evenly throughout.

ABOUT TIMING

Time is an important element in microwave cooking. But isn't that statement true for all cooking? You, the cook, have to be the judge, as you consider your family's preferences and use your own instincts. Be aware that even though the microwave oven is a superb product of computer technology, it is no more or less precise than any conventional cooking system. Nevertheless, because of the speed with which most food is cooked, timing is more crucial in microwave cooking than in conventional cooking. When you consider that a cooking task requiring one hour in a conventional oven generally needs only one-third, or less, of that time in a microwave oven, you can understand why, in microwave cooking, one minute can be the difference between overcooked or undercooked food. As a result, most microwave recipes express the probable minimum-maximum cooking times, as in "Cook on HI (max. power) 4 to 5 minutes." This direction is often assisted by a phrase such as "or until tender." As you become familiar with your oven you will recognize when to begin to check for doneness. Remember that it is better to undercook and add more cooking time than to overcook — then it's too late.

Cooking times might be precise if a way could be found to guarantee that all food would be exactly the same each time we cook it; if the utility company would guarantee not to alter our source of power (there are frequent changes in the voltage levels reaching our homes); and if the size, form, and content of food would be consistently the same. The fact is that one potato or one steak varies from another in density, moisture or fat content, shape, weight, and temperature. This is true of all food. The cook must be ready to adjust to the changes, to be flexible and observant. This discussion really comes down to the fact that you, not the microwave oven, are the cook. The oven can't make judgments, so you must. The recipes in this book have all been meticulously kitchen tested by expert home economists. You will find that the ranges of cooking times suggested are exact. As in all fine cooking,

however, microwave cooking needs and benefits from a personal touch.

CHARACTERISTICS THAT AFFECT TIMING

Many characteristics of food, such as quantity, shape, density, and starting temperature affect timing. Understanding them will help you become a skilled and successful microwave cook.

Quantity

The larger the volume of food there is, the more time is needed to cook it. For example, one potato may cook in 6 to 8 minutes but 2 potatoes take about one and a half times as long. If the quantity in a recipe is changed, be sure to make an adjustment in timing. When increasing a recipe, increase the amount of cooking time. Here is a general rule to follow: When doubling a recipe, increase the cooking time approximately 50 percent. When cutting a recipe in half, reduce the time by approximately 40 percent.

Density

Dense food such as potatoes, roast beef, and carrots takes longer to cook than porous food, such as cakes, ground beef, and apples, because it takes the microwaves longer to penetrate

Irregularly-shaped food requires special arrangement (above). Moist food cooks faster than dry (above left). Food areas close to the oven top are shielded during cooking (left).

the denser texture. For example, a 2-pound roast will take longer than a 2-pound meat loaf.

Height

As in conventional cooking, areas that are closer to the energy source cook faster. In most microwave ovens, the energy source is at the top of the oven. Food close to the top may require shielding with pieces of aluminum foil or turning for even cooking.

Shape and Size

Thin food cooks faster than thick food; thin sections faster than thick. Small pieces also cook faster than large pieces. For even

cooking, place thick pieces toward the outside of the dish, since the outside areas cook faster than the inside areas. For best results, try to cook pieces of similar size and shape together.

Moisture Content

Moist food cooks faster than dry food because microwave energy is easily absorbed by the moisture within the food. For example, 1 cup of sliced zucchini will cook faster than 1 cup of carrots because of the higher water content in the zucchini. In fact, the amount of free moisture within a food helps determine how rapidly it cooks.

Sugar and Fat Content

Food high in sugar and fat heats quicker than items low in these ingredients because microwave energy is attracted by sugar and fat. For example, the fruit or cheese filling of a sweet roll will heat faster than the roll itself and will be hotter, since sugar and fat reach higher temperatures than food low in sugar or fat content.

Delicate Ingredients

This term is used to refer to food that cooks so quickly in the microwave oven that it can overcook and toughen, separate, or curdle. For example, mayonnaise, cheese, eggs, cream, dairy sour cream, etc. Other food may "pop," such as snails, oysters, and chicken livers. For this reason, a lower power setting is often recommended for proper cooking. However, when these ingredients are mixed with other food, as in a casserole, stew, or soup, you may use a higher power setting, because volume automatically slows down the cooking.

Starting Temperature

As in conventional cooking, the temperature at which food is placed in the microwave oven affects the length of cooking time. More time is needed to cook food just out of the refrigerator than food at room temperature. For example, it takes longer to heat frozen green beans than canned green beans. Also, hot tap water will start boiling sooner than cold. Recipes in this book start with food at its normal storage temperature.

ABOUT UTENSILS

A wide variety of cookware and cooking implements can be used in the microwave oven. In order to indicate an item made of material that is safe and recommended for microwave cooking, we have created a new term, *microproof.* The Materials Checklist and Microproof Utensils Chart on the following pages will aid you in selecting the appropriate microproof utensil. Except for metal, most materials are microproof for at least a limited amount of cooking time. But unless specifically approved, items made of metal, even partially, are never to be used in the microwave oven, because they reflect microwaves, preventing them from passing through the cooking utensil into the food. In addition, metal that touches the oven sides will cause sparks, a static charge, known as arcing. Arcing is not harmful to you, though it will deface the oven. Metal twist ties or dishes or cups with gold or silver trim should not be used. See the Materials Checklist for those approved types of metal, such as pieces of aluminum foil, used as a shield over certain areas of food to prevent overcooking, or metal clips attached to frozen turkey.

When selecting a new piece of cookware, first check the manufacturer's directions. Also review the Materials Checklist and the Microproof Utensils Chart. If you are still in doubt, try this test: Pour a cup of water into a glass measure and place it in the oven next to the container or dish to be tested. Use HI (max. power) and cook for 1 minute. If the new dish feels hot, don't use it — it is absorbing microwave energy. If it feels warm, the dish may only be used for warming food. If it remains at room temperature, it is *microproof.*

The rapid growth of microwave cooking has created many new products for use in the microwave oven. Among these are microproof replacements for cookware formerly available only in metal. You'll find a wide variety at your store — cake, bundt, and muffin pans, roasting racks, etc. When you add these to traditional microproof cookware and the array of microproof plastic and paper products, you'll find that microwave cooking enables you to select from many more kinds of cookware than available for conventional cooking.

Selecting Containers

Containers should accommodate the food being cooked. And you must make sure that they fit in your oven. For best results, try to use the particular size or shape of dish cited in a recipe. Varying the container size or shape may change cooking time.

Whenever possible use round or oval dishes. Square corners in cookware receive more microwaves than the rest of the dish, so food in the corners tends to overcook. Some cake and loaf recipes call for ring molds or bundt pans to facilitate more even cooking. This is because the center area in a round or oval dish generally cooks more slowly than the outside. Round cookware with a small glass inserted open end up in the center also eliminates undercooked centers.

A 2-quart casserole called for in a recipe refers to a bowl-shaped cooking utensil. A 6×9-inch or a 9-inch round baking dish refers to a shallow cooking dish. In the case of puddings, sauces, and candies, fairly large containers are specified to prevent boiling over.

Materials Checklist

☐ CHINA, POTTERY: Ideal for microwave use. However, if they have metallic trim or glaze, they are not microproof and should not be used.

☐ GLASS: An excellent microwave cooking material. Especially useful for baking pies to check doneness of pie shells through the bottom. Since ovenproof glass is always safe, "microproof" is not mentioned in any recipe where a glass item is specified.

☐ METALS: *Not* suitable except as follows:

Small strips of aluminum foil can be used to cover areas on large pieces of meat or poultry that defrost or cook more rapidly than the rest of the piece — for example, a roast with jagged areas or thin ends, or the wing or breastbone of poultry. This method is known as *shielding* in microwave cooking.

Shallow aluminum TV dinner trays with foil covers removed can be heated, provided that the trays do not exceed 3/4 inch depth. However, this method only provides heating from the top, since the microwaves cannot penetrate the sides or bottom of the metal tray. It's best to "pop" the blocks of food out and place them on a dinner plate.

Frozen poultry containing metal clamps may be defrosted in the microwave oven without removing the clamps. Remove the clamps after defrosting.

Trays or any foil or metal item must be at least 1 inch from oven walls.

☐ PAPER: Approved for short-term cooking and for reheating. White paper towels, waxed paper, and parchment are suitable coverings. Extended use may cause the paper to burn. Must not be foil lined.

☐ PLASTICS: Excellent products have been designed for microwave use. Use plastics marked for microwave use and follow the directions of the manufacturer. Plastics that melt from the heat of the food should not be used.

☐ PLASTIC COOKING POUCHES: Can be used. Slit the pouch so steam can escape.

☐ STRAW AND WOOD: Can be used for quick warming. Be certain no metal is used on the straw or wood items.

Browning Dishes

A browning dish is used to sear, grill, fry, or brown food. It is made to absorb microwave energy. A special coating on the bottom of the dish becomes very hot when preheated in the microwave oven. For best results, follow the dish manufacturer's instructions.

After the dish is preheated, vegetable oil or butter may be added to enhance the browning and prevent food from sticking. After the food is placed on the preheated browning dish, the microwaves cook the interior of the food while the hot surface of the dish browns the exterior. The food is then turned over to brown the other side. The longer you wait to turn the food, the less browning occurs, since the dish cools off rapidly. You may need to drain the dish, wipe it, and preheat it again. Since the browning dish becomes very hot, be sure to use potholders.

Familiar items, such as muffin pans and molds, are available in microproof material. Other items, such as bacon racks and browning dishes, have been developed for microwave cooking (above). All kinds of paper products and many plastic ones make microwave cooking easy (above left). A wide variety of glass, ceramic, and wood products are perfect for microwave use (left).

A GUIDE TO MICROPROOF COOKWARE

ITEM	GOOD USE	GENERAL NOTES
China plates, cups	Heating dinners and drinks.	No metal trim.
Cooking pouches (plastic)	Cooking meat, vegetables, rice, other frozen food.	Slit pouch so steam can escape.
Corelle®	Heating dinners, soups, drinks.	Closed-handle cups should not be used.
Corning Ware® or Pyrex casseroles	Cooking main dishes, vegetables, desserts.	No metal trim.
Microwave browning dishes or grills	Searing, grilling, and frying small meat items; grilling sandwiches; frying eggs.	These utensils are specially made to absorb microwaves and preheat to high temperatures. They brown food that otherwise would not brown in a microwave oven.
Microwave roasting racks	Cooking roasts and chickens, squash and potatoes.	Special racks are available for cooking bacon.
Oven film and cooking bags	Cooking roasts or stews.	Substitute string for metal twist ties. Bag itself will not cause tenderizing. Do not use film with foil edges.
Paper plates, cups, napkins	Heating hot dogs, drinks, rolls, appetizers, sandwiches.	Absorbs moisture from baked goods and freshens them. Paper plates and cups with wax coatings should not be used.
Plastic wrap	Covering dishes.	Fold back edge to ventilate, allowing steam to escape.
Pottery and earthenware plates, mugs, etc.	Heating dinners, soups, drinks.	Some pottery has a metallic glaze. To check, use dish test (page 13).
Soft plastics, sherbet cartons	Reheating leftovers.	Used for very short reheating periods.
Thermometers	Measuring temperature of meat, poultry, and candy.	Use only approved microproof meat or candy thermometer in microwave oven.
TV dinner trays (aluminum)	Frozen dinners or homemade dinners.	No deeper than $\frac{3}{4}$ inch. Food will receive heat from top surface only. Foil covering food must be removed.
Waxed paper	Covering casseroles. Use as a tent.	Prevents splattering. Helps contain heat where a tight seal is not required. Food temperature may cause some melting.
Wooden spoons, wooden skewers, straw baskets	Stirring puddings and sauces; for shish kabobs, appetizers, warming breads.	Can withstand microwaves for short cooking periods. Be sure no metal fittings on wood or straw.

ABOUT METHODS

The evenness and speed of microwave cooking are affected not only by the characteristics of food but also by certain cooking methods. Some of these techniques are used in conventional cooking as well, but they are particularly important with microwave cooking. Many other important variables are included here.

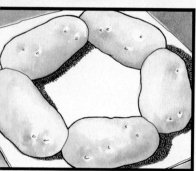

Microwave arrangement methods create unique cook-and-serve opportunities, such as the vegetable platter above. Chicken legs look like the spokes in a wheel.

Arrangement

The way food is arranged in the dish and in the oven enhances even cooking and speeds defrosting and cooking food. Microwaves penetrate the outer portion of food first; therefore, food should be arranged so that the denser, thicker areas are near the dish edge, and the thinner, more porous areas are near the center. For example, when cooking broccoli, split the heavy stalks to expose more area, then overlap florets. Chicken legs are arranged like the spokes of a wheel, with the bony end toward the center. This gives even density to the food and provides even cooking. Place shrimp in a ring with the tails toward the center. Food such as cupcakes or potatoes should be arranged in a circle, not in rows.

Turning Over

As in conventional cooking, some food, such as large roasts, whole poultry, a ham, or hamburgers, may require turning over to brown each side and to promote even heating. Any food seared on the browning dish should be turned over. During the defrosting process in the microwave oven, it is often necessary to turn food.

Rotating

Some food, such as pies and cakes, that cannot be stirred, turned over, or rearranged, calls for repositioning the cooking dish one-quarter turn to allow for even distribution of the microwave energy. Rotate only if the baked food is not cooking or rising evenly. Most food does not need to be rotated.

Turning (above), rotating (above left), and stirring (left) assist in even cooking.

Stirring

Less stirring is required in microwave cooking than in conventional cooking. When necessary, stir from the outside to the center, since the outside heats faster than the center portion. Stirring blends the flavors and promotes even heating. Stir only as directed in the recipes. Constant stirring is never required in microwave cooking

Rearranging

Sometimes food that cannot be stirred needs repositioning in the cooking utensil to allow even heating. When rearranging food, move the center food to the outside of the dish and the outer food toward the center.

Piercing

It is essential to pierce the skin or membrane of certain food, such as egg yolks, potatoes, liver, eggplant, and squash. Because they retain moisture during cook- ing, they must be pierced to prevent bursting and to allow steam to escape. A toothpick may be used for egg yolks; a fork is best for potatoes and squash.

Types of covers for microwave cooking (above). Piercing is important with certain food (above right). The effect of standing time on a beef roast (right).

Covering

Covers are used to trap steam, prevent dehydration, speed cooking, and help food retain its natural moisture. Suitable tight coverings are microproof casserole tops, glass covers, plastic wraps, oven bags, and microproof plates and saucers. Remove coverings away from your face to prevent steam burns. Paper toweling is especially useful as a light covering to prevent splatter and to absorb moisture. Waxed paper helps retain heat and moisture.

Standing Time

This term refers to the time food needs to complete cooking or thawing after the microwave time has ended. During standing time, heat continues to be conducted from the outside to the center of the food. After the oven is turned off, food may remain in the oven for standing time or may be placed on a heatproof counter. This procedure is an essential part of food preparation with the microwave oven. Some food, such as roasts, requires standing time to attain the proper internal temperature for rare, medium, or well-done. Casseroles need standing time to allow the heat to spread evenly and to complete reheating or cooking. With cakes, pies, and quiches, standing time permits the center to finish cooking. During the standing time outside the oven, place food on a flat surface, such as a heat-resistant breadboard or counter top, not on a cooling rack as you would conventionally.

Shielding

Certain thin or bony areas, such as the wing tips of poultry, the head and tail of fish, or the breastbone of a turkey, cook faster than thicker areas. Covering these parts with small pieces of aluminum foil shields these areas from overcooking, since aluminum foil reflects the waves. Be careful not to allow the foil to touch the oven walls.

Browning

Many foods do not brown in the microwave oven as much as they do in the conventional oven. Depending upon the fat content, most food will brown in 8 to 10 minutes in the microwave oven. For example, bacon browns in minutes because of its high fat content. For food that cooks too quickly to brown, such as ham-

burgers, fried eggs, steak or cutlets, a special browning dish is available. A longer cooking time, or higher fat content will provide more browning. You can also create a browned look by brushing on a browning agent, such as gravy mix, onion soup mix, etc. Cakes, bread, and pie shells do not brown. Using chocolate, spices, or dark flour helps attain the dark color. Or you can create appealing color by adding frostings or dark spices.

High Altitude Adjustments

As in conventional cooking, microwave cooking at high altitudes requires adjustments in cooking time for leavened products like bread and cake. Other foods may require a slightly longer cooking time to become tender, since water boils at a lower temperature. Usually, for every 3 minutes of microwave cooking time you add 1 minute for the higher altitude. Therefore, a recipe calling for 3 minutes needs 4 minutes and a recipe requiring 6 minutes needs 8 minutes. The wisest procedure is to start with the time given in the recipe and then check for doneness. Adding time is easy, but overcooking can be a real problem.

GETTING TO KNOW YOUR OVEN

Your microwave oven gives you the ability to select from many power settings in graduated form from zero to 100 percent — HI (max. power). Just as in a conventional oven, these settings give you flexibility and the necessary control to produce perfectly cooked dishes. You can set your multi-power oven to suit the foods being cooked. Many foods require slow cooking at less than full power to achieve the best results. In addition to HI (max. power) there are 99 multi-power settings. Each recipe in the book indicates which power setting is recommended for the food being cooked. The following chart outlines the specific uses for the main settings.

Guide for Power Control Settings

Settings	Suggested Cooking Uses
1	Keeping casseroles and main dishes warm.
20 (warm)	Softening cream cheese.
35 (low)	Softening chocolate; heating breads, rolls pancakes, and tacos; clarifying butter; taking chill out of fruit; heating small amounts of food.
50 (defrost)	Thawing meat, poultry, and seafood; finish cooking certain casseroles, stews, and some sauces.
60 (braise)	Cooking less tender cuts of meat in liquid and slow-cooking dishes; finish cooking less tender roasts.
75 (simmer)	Cooking stews and soups; cooking custards and pasta.
90 (bake)	Cooking scrambled eggs; cakes.
HI (roast)	Cooking rump roast, ham, veal, and lamb; cooking cheese dishes; cooking eggs, meatloaf, and milk; cooking quick breads and cereal products.
HI (reheat)	Quickly reheating precooked or prepared foods; heating sandwiches.
HI (sauté)	Quickly cooking onions, celery, and green peppers; reheating meat slices.
HI (max. power)	Cooking tender cuts of meat; cooking poultry, fish, vegetables, and most casseroles; preheating the browning dish; boiling water; cooking muffins.

Internal Temperature

As in conventional cooking, the most accurate way to gauge doneness is with a food thermometer. However, you *cannot use a conventional meat thermometer* with the microwave oven because it may cause sparks, a static charge, known as arcing. Arcing is not harmful to you, though it will deface the oven. Specially designed food thermometers are available for microwave use and some can also be used in your conventional oven. Carefully check the thermometer manufacturer's instructions.

The "Guide to Internal Temperatures" provides a range from 120°F to 180°F. Keep in mind that standing time is essential for most food to reach its optimum serving temperature and quality. So, the temperatures in the Guide are 5 to 15 degrees *below* the desired ready-to-carve or eat internal temperature. Because of

Specially designed microwave food thermometers are a valuable aid to accurate determination of doneness.

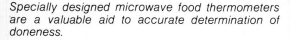

the nature of microwave energy, during standing time the temperature of most food rises about 5° to 15°F. For example, after 10 minutes of standing time, the temperature of rare beef will reach 140°F; well done lamb will reach its proper 170° to 180°F.

Guide to Internal Temperatures

Suggested Thermometer Readings	
120°	Rare Beef, Precooked Ham
130°	Medium Beef
140°	Fish Steaks and Fillets, Well Done Beef
150°	Vegetables,Hot Drinks, Soups, Casseroles
155°	Veal
165°	Well Done Lamb, Pork
170°	Poultry Parts, Whole Fish
180°	Well Done Whole Poultry

Thermometer Use

As in conventional cooking, the thermometer must be carefully and properly inserted in the food to obtain the best results. Do not allow the thermometer — and, again, remember we are talking about a *special microwave thermometer* — to touch bone or fat. False readings may result. Here are a few tips.

☐ For *roasts*, place the thermometer in the roast about equal distance between the ends. The tip should be inserted until it reaches the approximate center of the meat.

☐ For *poultry*, place the thermometer between the body and the inner thigh. Avoid bone.

☐ Check *defrosting* food with the thermometer. If the dial drops to a lower temperature or the thermometer cannot be inserted, you know that the food has not reached room temperature or is still frozen.

☐ In *reheating* food, a microwave thermometer can be valuable to obtain exact temperatures for casseroles, soups, and leftovers. (150°F to 170°F are good temperature guides for soups, casseroles, etc.)

☐ In *candy making*, temperature checks are especially helpful. You can obtain microproof candy thermometers but keep in mind that space in the oven is limited. You can check candy mixture temperatures *outside the oven* with a conventional candy thermometer.

Reheating

One of the major assets of the microwave oven is its efficiency in reheating cooked food. Not only does most food reheat quickly, but it also retains moisture and its just-cooked flavor when properly arranged and covered. If someone is late for dinner, there's no need to fret. Just place a microproof plate containing the cooked food in your oven; in moments, dinner is ready once again. Reheat food in serving dishes or on paper plates and save extra cleanup time. Take-out food, which usually arrives at your home cooled off, can be easily reheated in seconds to its original state in your microwave oven. No more cold pizzas or lukewarm hamburgers. Leftovers are a treat, too. You may even want to prepare food the day before, refrigerate, and serve the following day. You'll no longer call food leftovers, because it will taste as if "just made." Follow the tips below to help get excellent results when you are reheating food.

☐ To arrange a combination of different foods on a plate, place the dense food, like meat, at the outer edges and the more porous food, like breads, toward the center. Food that cooks most quickly should be placed at the center, with slower cooking food at the edges.

☐ Dense food, such as mashed potatoes and casseroles, cooks more quickly and evenly if a depression is made in the center, or if the food is shaped in a ring.

☐ To retain moisture during reheating, cover food with plastic wrap or a microproof lid. Wrap breads and sandwiches in paper toweling to absorb moisture and prevent sogginess. Use waxed paper to hold heat in and still allow steam to escape.

☐ Spread food out in a shallow container rather than piling it high, for quicker and more even heating.

☐ As a general guide to reheating a plate of food, start with 1½ to 2 minutes on HI (max. power), then check for doneness. If the plate on which the food is cooked feels warm, the food is probably heated through, for its warmth has heated the plate. Because of the numerous variables in the food to be reheated, i.e., amount, shape, food characteristics, starting temperature, etc., recommended times can only be approximate.

Defrosting

One of the great attractions of the microwave oven is its ability to defrost raw food or heat frozen cooked food. You need only to choose 50 (defrost) for most food and observe the swiftness and ease of defrosting. The few exceptions are provided in the Defrosting Guides at the beginning of some chapters.

Many of the same principles and techniques that apply to microwave cooking also apply to microwave defrosting. Microwaves are attracted to water or moisture molecules. As soon as microwaves have defrosted a portion of the item, they are more attracted to the thawed portion. The frozen portion continues to thaw, but this is due to the heat in the thawed portion. Special techniques, such as shielding and rotating, are helpful to be sure the thawed portion does not cook before the rest defrosts. It is often necessary to turn, stir, and separate to assist the defrosting process. Defrosting requires standing time to complete. Because food differs in size, weight, and density, recommended defrosting times can only be approximate. Additional standing time may be necessary to defrost

Many foods can begin defrosting in their original wrappers (above). Remove thawed portions of ground beef so that cooking does not start. Fish fillets and thin meat slices should be separated as soon as possible (right).

completely. Read the Defrosting Guides throughout the book for times and special instructions about defrosting specific foods. Here are some tips to aid you toward fast and easy defrosting.

☐ Remove poultry, seafood, fish, and meat from their original closed package and place on dish to provide more even thawing and to prevent partial cooking from steam that could be produced in the sealed package. You may leave metal clips in poultry during defrosting, but you should remove them as soon as possible before cooking. Replace metal twists on bags with string or rubber bands before defrosting.

☐ Plastic-wrapped packages from the supermarket meat department may not be wrapped with a plastic wrap recommended for microwave use. If in doubt, unwrap package and place food on a microproof plate.

☐ Vegetables are usually packaged to go right into the microwave for defrosting and heating to serving temperature. Vegetables packaged in foil should be removed from package and placed in microproof dish. Pierce vegetables in plastic pouches to allow steam to escape. It is not necessary to use the 55 (defrost) setting for frozen vegetables. They are prepared on HI (max. power).

☐ Poultry wings, legs, and the small or bony ends of meat or fish may need to be covered with pieces of aluminum foil for part of the thawing time to prevent cooking while the remainder thaws.

☐ Large items should be turned and rotated halfway through defrosting time to provide more even thawing.

☐ Food textures influence thawing time. Because of air space, porous food like bread defrosts more quickly than a solid mass, such as a roast.

☐ The edges will begin cooking if meat, fish, and seafood are completely thawed in the microwave oven. Therefore, food should still be icy in the center when removed from oven. It will finish thawing while standing.

☐ To thaw half of a frozen vegetable package, wrap half the package with aluminum foil. When unwrapped side is thawed, separate and return balance to freezer.

☐ Thin or sliced items, such as fish fillets, meat patties, etc., should be separated as soon as possible. Remove thawed pieces and allow others to continue thawing.

☐ Casseroles, saucy foods, vegetables, and soups should be stirred once or twice during defrosting to redistribute heat.

☐ Frozen fried foods may be defrosted but will not be crisp when heated in the microwave oven.

☐ Freezing tips: It is helpful to freeze in small quantities rather than in one large piece. When freezing casseroles, it's a good idea to insert an empty paper cup in the center so no food is present there. This speeds thawing. Depressing the center of ground meat before freezing also hastens thawing later. Take care to wrap and package food well.

LET'S USE THE OVEN

Now it's time for some practical experience using all the features of your microwave oven: first, a quick hot drink, then, a scrambled egg. Let's begin.

Lesson One

A quick pick-me-up

Take your favorite mug or cup; be sure there is no gold or silver trim or metallic glaze. If you are not certain if your mug is microproof, test it as directed on page 13. Then follow these step-by-step directions:

1. Fill mug with water and place in the center of the oven. Close the oven door.

2. Touch "Clear" pad to clear any previous programming. (This is not a necessary step if there is no previous programming.)

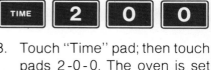

3. Touch "Time" pad; then touch pads 2-0-0. The oven is set for 2 minutes on HI (max. power). (The oven will automatically cook on HI (max. power) unless a lower setting is entered.)

4. Now touch "Start" pad.

5. The timer will beep when 2 minutes have passed. The oven turns off automatically. Open the door.

6. Remove the mug. The handle will be cool enough to hold and the mug itself will be warm from the water. Stir in instant coffee, tea, or soup and enjoy!

4. Touch "Start" pad.

5. When 30 seconds have passed, oven will "beep." Open oven door. Stir egg mixture briskly. Return to oven; close door.

Lesson Two
Scrambled Egg

1. Break egg into a microproof bowl or 2-cup glass measure. Add 1 tablespoon milk. Beat with a fork. Add 1 teaspoon butter or margarine.

2. Cover with waxed paper. Place in oven and close door.

6. Touch "Time" pad; then touch pads 1-0-0. Oven is set to cook for 1 minute on HI (max. power).

7. Touch "Start" pad. Oven will "beep" and turn off automatically when cooking time ends.

8. Let egg stand 1 minute before serving — just time to prepare juice and a sweet roll.

3. Touch "Clear" pad; touch "Time" pad; then touch pads 3 and 0. The oven is set for 30 seconds on HI (max. power).

Lesson Three
Juice and Sweet Roll

1. Spoon frozen juice into a 4-cup glass measure or microproof serving pitcher, and place in oven. Close door.

2. Touch "Clear" pad; touch "Time" pad; then touch pads 3 and 0. The oven is set for 30 seconds on HI (max. power).

3. Touch "Start."

4. When the timer "beeps" open door and remove container. Add water and stir briskly.

5. Set sweet roll on paper plate or paper napkin.

6. Place in oven and close door.

7. Touch "Clear" pad; touch "Time" pad; then touch pads 3 and 0. Touch "Cook Control" pad, then pads 3 and 5. The oven is set for 30 seconds on 35 (low) setting.

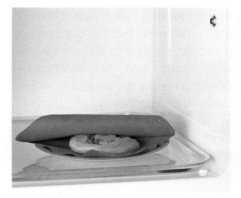

8. Touch "Start" pad. Bakery products should be only warm to the touch, since they will be hotter just below the surface. Because microwaves are attracted to sugar, the frosting or jelly may be very hot.

9. Enjoy your breakfast!

ON YOUR OWN

You will undoubtedly want to cook some of your favorite conventional recipes in the microwave oven. With a little thought and experimenting, you can convert many recipes. Before converting a recipe, study it to determine if it will adapt well to microwave cooking. Look for a recipe in the book that matches your conventional one most closely. For example, find a recipe with the same amount, type, and form of main ingredient, such as 1 pound ground meat or 2 pounds beef cut in 1-inch pieces, etc. Then compare other ingredients, such as pasta or vegetables. The microwave recipe will probably call for less liquid, because there is so little evaporation in microwave cooking. At the beginning of each recipe chapter hints on adapting recipes are provided. Also use the following guidelines:

☐ Candies, bar cookies, meatloaf, and certain baked goods may not need adjustments in ingredients. For your puddings, cakes, sauces, gravies, and certain casseroles, liquids should be reduced.

☐ Most converted recipes will require adjustments in cooking time. Although a "rule of thumb" always has exceptions, you can generally assume that most microwave recipes are heated in about one-quarter to one-third of the conventional recipe time. Check for doneness after one-quarter of the time before continuing to cook.

Cooking Casseroles

The microwave oven is exceptionally good for cooking casseroles. Here are some general hints to help you:

☐ Most casseroles can be made ahead of time, refrigerated or frozen, then reheated later in the microwave.

☐ Many casseroles will require adjustment in the order in which ingredients are added. Certain ingredients, such as long-grain rice, take longer to cook than others. When converting to microwave, substitute a quicker-cooking ingredient, such as precooked rice, or substitute instant onion flakes for chopped onion.

☐ Casseroles are usually covered with plastic wrap or glass lids during cooking.

☐ Allow casseroles to stand 5 to 10 minutes before serving, according to size. Standing time completes cooking of the casserole center.

☐ You will obtain best results if you make ingredients uniform in size, stirring occasionally to distribute heat. If the ingredients are of different sizes, stir more often.

☐ Casseroles containing less tender meat need longer simmering. Those work well on 50 (defrost) which gives a slow-cooker effect. Cheese toppings should be added for the last 1 or 2 minutes.

☐ When used in quick-cooking casseroles, celery, onions, green peppers, and carrots should be sautéed before being added to dish. Rice or noodles should be partially cooked before combining with cooked meat, fish, or poultry.

About Lower Calories

Scattered throughout the book are low-calorie suggestions and low-calorie recipes. They are listed in the index so you can find them when you need them. In general, you can lower calories in many recipes by making substitutions such as these:

☐ Bouillon or water for butter when sautéing or softening vegetables.

☐ Vegetables for potatoes or pasta.

☐ Lean meats for fatty ones.

☐ Skim milk for whole milk.

☐ Skim milk cheeses like low-fat cottage, ricotta, and mozzarella for creamy fatty ones.

☐ Natural gravy with herbs for cream and butter sauces.

☐ Skinless chicken breast for regular cut-up chicken.

By the Way . . .

To get the greatest pleasure out of your microwave oven, keep in mind that certain food is best done by conventional means of cooking. For the following reasons, we don't recommend:

☐ Eggs cooked in the shell, because the light membrane surrounding the yolk collects energy, which then causes a steam build-up that will explode the egg. Don't experiment. It's a mess to clean up!

☐ Deep-fat frying, because the confined environment of the oven is not suited to the handling of the food or oil and is not safe.

☐ Pancakes, because no crust forms. (But the oven is great for reheating pancakes, waffles, and similar items.)

☐ Toasting, because it also requires crust development.

☐ Home canning, because it is impossible to judge exact boiling temperatures inside the jars and you cannot be sure that the temperature and cooking time are sufficient to prevent contamination.

☐ Chiffon and angel food cakes, because they require steady, dry heat to rise and be tender.

☐ Heating bottles with small necks, like those for syrups and toppings, because they are apt to break from the pressure build-up.

☐ Large items, such as a 25-pound turkey or a dozen baking potatoes, because the space is not adequate and no time is saved.

☐ True soufflés, because the microwaves tend to make dishes high in egg content a bit rubbery.

About popcorn:

Do not attempt to pop corn in a paper bag, since the corn may dehydrate and overheat, causing the paper bag to catch on fire. Due to the many variables, such as the age of the corn and its moisture content, popping corn in the microwave oven is not recommended. Microwave popping devices are available. While safe to use, they usually do not give results equal to those of conventional popping methods. If the microwave device is used, *carefully follow the instructions provided with the product.*

STARTERS AND SNACKS

Tangy Beef Balls (page 39) and Nacho Rounds (page 42) are arranged in the circular microwave pattern (left). Arrange drinks the same way (above).

Whether you choose to call them tidbits, snacks, or appetizers, they always rate high with the family and guests. The incredible speed of the microwave oven makes all the last-minute hustle and hassle disappear. You can really be part of the party!

Start off a special family meal with Tomato Jalapeño Cheese Dip (page 40) or Olive and Bacon Wraps (page 42). If you want to surprise friends during the next "come-on-over" night, Chicken Wings Canton (page 40) and Party Franks (page 38) will surely make them wonder where you found the time to fuss.

Hot drinks are in this chapter, too, because they sure can make any snack a special treat.

And how about those days when the kids drag in from school, so down in the dumps that you don't know what to do? Perk up their day with Muffin Toppers (page 36) and a friendly mug of our Hot Chocolate Malt (page 36).

Converting Your Recipes

Most of your favorite hot appetizers will adapt well to micro-wave cooking, except those wrapped in pastry. Pastry requires the hot environment of the conventional oven to become crisp.

The recipe for Olive and Bacon Wraps (page 42) is an ideal guide for countless appetizers containing seafood, chicken, vegetable, and fruit combinations. Here are some tips:

☐ Toppings for canapés can be made ahead but do not place on bread or crackers until just before heating. This assures a crisp base.
☐ Cover appetizers or dips only when the recipe specifies doing so. Use fitted glass lids, waxed paper, plastic wrap, or paper towels.
☐ Compare your favorite dip recipe with one of the choices here to determine your microwave time.
☐ While the microwave oven is not recommended for baking pastry appetizers, it is perfect for reheating such items.

COOKING GUIDE — CONVENIENCE APPETIZERS

Food	Amount	Power Control Setting	Time	Special Notes
Canned meat spread	4 oz.	HI (max. power)	45 - 60 seconds	Transfer to small microproof bowl.
Canned sausages, cocktail sausages	5 oz.	HI (max. power)	1½ - 2 minutes	Place in covered glass casserole.
Cocktail franks, pizza roll	4 servings	HI (max. power)	1 - 1½ minutes	Place on paper towels. Roll will not crisp.
Cooked pizza, 10 inches, cut in 8 portions	1 wedge	HI (max. power)	1 - 1½ minutes	Place on paper towels or paper plate or leave in uncovered cardboard box, points toward center.
	4 wedges	HI (max. power)	2 - 3 minutes	
	Whole	HI (max. power)	4 - 5 minutes	
Dips, cream	½ cup	20 (warm)	30 - 50 seconds	Cover with plastic wrap.
Eggrolls, pastry-covered	2 servings	HI (max. power)	40 - 60 seconds	Place on paper towels, do not cover.
Swiss fondue, frozen	10 oz.	HI (max. power)	6 - 7½ minutes	Slit pouch. Place on micro-proof plate. Stir once.

COOKING GUIDE — HOT DRINKS

Liquid	Power Control Setting	6-ounce Cup	Time (minutes)	8-ounce Cup	Time (minutes)	Special Notes
Water	HI (max. power)	1	$1\frac{1}{2}$-2	1	$2\frac{1}{2}$-$2\frac{3}{4}$	For instant coffee, soup, tea, etc.
		2	$2\frac{1}{2}$-3	2	$3\frac{1}{2}$-4	
Milk	HI (max. power)	1	$1\frac{1}{2}$-2	1	2-$2\frac{1}{2}$	For cocoa, etc.
		2	$2\frac{1}{2}$-$3\frac{1}{2}$	2	$3\frac{1}{2}$-4	
Reheating coffee	HI (max. power)	1	$1\frac{1}{2}$-$1\frac{3}{4}$	1	$1\frac{1}{2}$-2	
		2	$2\frac{1}{4}$-$2\frac{3}{4}$	2	3-$3\frac{1}{2}$	

Deviled Ham Triangles ——————— 14 servings

Total Cooking Time: 3 to 4 minutes

7 slices white or whole
    wheat bread
1 can ($4\frac{1}{2}$ ounces)
    deviled ham
2 teaspoons Burgundy
    Dash freshly ground
    pepper
1 egg white
3 tablespoons mayonnaise
1 teaspoon dry mustard
    Paprika

Trim crusts from bread; toast. Cut toast diagonally into triangles. In small bowl, combine ham, Burgundy, and pepper; blend well. Spread on toast triangles. In small mixing bowl, beat egg white until stiff; fold in mayonnaise and mustard. Spread over ham mixture. Place half of the triangles in circle on paper towel-lined microproof plate. Cook on HI (max. power) $1\frac{1}{2}$ to 2 minutes, or until egg white is set, rotating plate once. Repeat with remaining triangles. Sprinkle each serving with dash of paprika.

Beef Muffin Toppers ——————— 2 servings

Total Cooking Time: 2 minutes

$\frac{1}{3}$ cup lean ground beef
1 English muffin, split and
    toasted
$\frac{1}{2}$ teaspoon garlic powder
$\frac{1}{4}$ teaspoon salt
    Dash freshly ground
    pepper
$\frac{1}{4}$ cup shredded Cheddar or
    1 slice processed
    Cheddar cheese, halved

Divide beef and spread with a knife on muffin halves. Sprinkle garlic powder, salt, and pepper evenly on muffin halves. Place on microproof plate. Cook on HI (max. power) 2 minutes. Sprinkle shredded cheese or place $\frac{1}{2}$ slice cheese on each serving. Let stand 1 minute, or until cheese is melted. Serve hot.

Hot Chocolate Malt _____ 4 servings

Total Cooking Time: 5 to 6 minutes

2 cups milk
¼ cup chocolate syrup
4 tablespoons instant malted
milk powder

In 4-cup glass measure, combine all ingredients. Cook on HI (max. power) 5 to 6 minutes, or until hot, stirring once during cooking time. Serve in warm mugs.

For a quick cup of hot chocolate, pour 1 cup chocolate milk into mug. Stir in 2 tablespoons instant malted milk powder. Cook on HI (max. power) 1½ to 2 minutes.

Muffin Toppers _____ 2 servings

Total Cooking Time: 2 minutes

1 tablespoon butter or
margarine
½ teaspoon prepared mustard
1 English muffin, split and
toasted
½ cup chopped or 2 slices
cooked ham
½ cup shredded cheese
(Swiss, mozzarella,
Cheddar, or Monterey
Jack)

Thoroughly blend butter and mustard; spread on muffin halves. Divide ham between muffins. Top with cheese. Place on microproof plate. Cook on 50 (defrost) 2 minutes. Let stand 1 minute before serving.

Leftover cooked meat or poultry can also be used for toppers. Thinly slice or cube and pile on muffins. Try adding sauerkraut, pickles, or toppings of your choice.

For 4 servings, place muffins in a circle on microproof plate. Cook on 50 (defrost) 4 minutes.

Chili Bean Dip _____ 2 cups

Total Cooking Time: 5 to 8 minutes

1 can (15 ounces) chili
   with beans
8 ounces process American
   cheese, diced
2 drops hot pepper sauce

Place chili in container of blender. Cover and process until smooth. Pour into 1½-quart microproof bowl. Add cheese and hot pepper sauce. Cook on 50 (defrost) 5 to 8 minutes, or until cheese is melted, stirring once during cooking time. Blend well. Serve with corn or tortilla chips.

Party Franks _____ 10 to 12 servings

Total Cooking Time: 9½ minutes

1½ pounds frankfurters
  1 jar (10 ounces) cranberry
     jelly
  2 tablespoons prepared
     mustard

Cut each frankfurter crosswise into 4 sections. Cut each section in half lengthwise to make 8 pieces. Split ends of each piece within ¼-inch of the center; set aside. Combine jelly and mustard in 2-quart microproof casserole. Cook on 50 (defrost) 5 minutes, or until jelly is melted, stirring after 3 minutes. Add frankfurters; stir to coat. Cover with waxed paper. Cook on HI (max. power) 2½ minutes, stir. Cook on HI (max. power) 2 minutes, or until hot. Stir and let stand, covered, 3 minutes. Serve with cocktail picks.

Spiced Cider _____ 1 quart

Total Cooking Time: 17 to 20 minutes

1 quart apple cider
¼ cup firmly packed light
   brown sugar
½ teaspoon whole cloves
½ teaspoon whole allspice
1 cinnamon stick
  Dash salt

Combine all ingredients in 2-quart microproof casserole. Cook on 50 (defrost) 17 to 20 minutes, or until hot. Remove spices. Serve hot, garnished with slices of red apple, if desired.

Tangy Beef Balls _____ 4 dozen
Total Cooking Time: 10 to 12 minutes

½ cup butter-flavored
    cracker crumbs
⅓ cup evaporated milk
¼ teaspoon salt
1 tablespoon instant minced
    onion
2 teaspoons curry powder
1 pound lean ground beef

Combine crumbs, milk, salt, onion, and curry; mix lightly. Add beef and blend thoroughly. Shape mixture into 48 1-inch balls. Arrange half of the balls in a double circle on a round microproof plate. Cover with waxed paper. Cook on HI (max. power) 5 to 6 minutes, or until beef is no longer red, rotating dish once during cooking time. Repeat with remaining meatballs. Serve on toothpicks.

If sauce is desired, melt 1 package (10 ounces) frozen Welsh Rabbit in 1-quart microproof casserole. Cook on HI (max. power) 5 to 6 minutes, or until hot, stirring as soon as melted and again during cooking time. Pour over meatballs, stirring to coat.

Roasted Soybean Nuts _____ 3½ cups
Total Cooking Time: 50 to 55 minutes

1 cup dried soybeans
2½ cups water
2 tablespoons vegetable
    oil
  Salt

Soak soybeans in water to cover overnight. Add additional water, if necessary. Drain. In 2-quart glass bowl, cover soybeans with 2½ cups water. Cook on HI (max. power) 30 minutes, or until soft; skim and stir every 5 minutes. Drain; spread on paper towels until dry. In 10-inch glass pie plate, mix half of the cooked soft beans with 1 tablespoon of the oil; stir to coat. Cook on HI (max. power) 20 to 25 minutes, or until crisp, stirring frequently, especially after 10 minutes. Spread on paper towels; sprinkle lightly with salt. Repeat with remaining beans and oil. Store in airtight container.

Chicken Wings Canton _____ 2 to 4 servings
Total Cooking Time: 16 to 17 minutes

6 chicken wings
1/4 · cup soy sauce
1/2 cup fine cracker crumbs
1/2 teaspoon garlic powder
1/2 teaspoon paprika
1/4 teaspoon ginger
1/8 teaspoon freshly ground
   pepper

Cut wings in half; discard tips, or save for use in chicken broth. Rinse; pat dry with paper towels. Pour soy sauce into shallow bowl; set aside. In another shallow bowl, combine remaining ingredients. Dip chicken in soy sauce; roll in seasoned crumbs, coating evenly. Arrange chicken wings, skin-side up in spoke pattern in 9-inch round glass pie plate, placing thickest portions toward outside of plate. Cover with paper towels. Cook on HI (max. power) 9 minutes. Rotate dish one-quarter turn. Cook on HI (max. power) 7 to 8 minutes, or until chicken is tender. Serve hot.

Tomato Jalapeño Cheese Dip _____ about 4 cups
Total Cooking Time: 7 to 10 minutes

2 pounds process American
   cheese, cubed
1 can (1 1/2 ounces) tomatoes
   and jalapeño peppers,
   drained
1 can (5 1/3 ounces)
   evaporated milk

Combine all ingredients in 2-quart microproof bowl. Cook on HI (max. power) 7 to 10 minutes, or until cheese is melted, stirring once during cooking time. Blend thoroughly with electric mixer. Pour into serving bowl. Serve with corn chips or dipping-style potato chips.

Extra dip can be frozen in plastic containers. To reheat, cook on 50 (defrost) 1 minute. Stir and repeat until dipping consistency.

Olive and Bacon Wraps —————— 2 dozen
Total Cooking Time: 26 to 28 minutes

12 slices bacon
 1 jar (4¾ ounces) large
      stuffed green olives,
      (about 24), drained
 2 tablespoons brown sugar,
      divided

Cut bacon slices in half. Wrap a piece of bacon around each olive, securing with a toothpick. Place half of the olives in a circle on a paper towel-lined microproof plate. Sprinkle with 1 tablespoon of sugar. Cover with a paper towel. Cook on HI (max. power) 10 minutes. Turn olives over. Cover. Cook on HI (max. power) 3 to 4 minutes, or until bacon is cooked. Let stand 1 minute before serving. Repeat with remaining olives.

Nacho Rounds —————— 4 to 6 servings
Total Cooking Time: 7 to 8 minutes

 1 package (8 ounces)
      tortilla chips
 2 cups shredded Cheddar
      cheese
 1 can (4 ounces) diced
      green chilies, drained
 1 can (2¼ ounces) chopped
      black olives, drained

Arrange chips on 2 10-inch microproof serving platters. Cover each with cheese, chilies, and olives. Cook on 50 (defrost), 1 plate at a time, 3½ to 4 minutes, or until cheese is melted. Rotate once during cooking time. Repeat with remaining plate.

Shrimp Cream Cheese Dip ——————— 2 cups
Total Cooking Time: 3½ to 4 minutes

1 package (8 ounces) cream
   cheese, quartered
1 can (7 ounces) broken
   shrimp, drained
2 tablespoons catsup or
   chili sauce
1 teaspoon instant minced
   onion
1 teaspoon prepared mustard
1 teaspoon Worcestershire
   sauce
¼ teaspoon garlic powder

Combine all ingredients in 1-quart microproof casserole. Cook on HI (max. power) 3½ to 4 minutes, or until warm, stirring once during cooking time. Stir; serve with crackers or chips.

To reduce calories, substitute low-fat Neufchatel for cream cheese and substitute raw vegetables for crackers or chips. Zucchini rounds are especially nice and can even be topped with the dip, as a spread.

Wine Warmer ————————————— 8 servings
Total Cooking Time: 6 minutes

⅕ gallon full-bodied red
   wine
3 teaspoons sugar
   Orange peel, cut in
   2-inch strips
2 cinnamon sticks

Combine all ingredients in 2-quart microproof bowl. Cook on 75 (simmer) 6 minutes. Do not boil. Serve in mugs garnished with an orange slice.

Liver Brandy Spread ————————— 3 cups
Total Cooking Time: 12 to 13 minutes

1 pound chicken livers,
   rinsed and drained
1 small onion, chopped
½ cup diced celery
¼ cup unsalted butter
1 clove garlic, halved
   Dash freshly ground
   pepper
2 tablespoons brandy
1 hard-cooked egg, chopped

Pierce livers in several places with toothpick. Combine livers, onion, celery, butter, garlic, and pepper in 2-quart microproof casserole. Cover. Cook on HI (max. power) 7 minutes, stirring once during cooking time. Cook, uncovered, on HI (max. power) 5 to 6 minutes, or until livers are no longer pink. Let stand, covered, 10 minutes. Purée liver mixture and brandy in container of electric blender or food processor. Pour into serving bowl. Sprinkle with egg. Chill thoroughly 3 to 4 hours, before serving.

Hot Crab and Sherry Dip _____ 2 cups
Total Cooking Time: 3½ to 4 minutes

1 package (8 ounces) cream cheese, quartered
2 tablespoons sherry
2 tablespoons milk
1 tablespoon instant minced onion
1½ teaspoons grated lemon rind
1 teaspoon horseradish
⅛ teaspoon garlic powder
1 can (7 ounces) crab meat, drained and flaked

Place cheese in 1-quart microproof casserole. Cook on HI (max. power) 1 to 1½ minutes, or until softened. Stir in remaining ingredients, except crab, until smooth. Stir in crab. Spread evenly in casserole. Cook on HI (max. power) 2½ minutes, or until warm. Stir. Sprinkle with paprika before serving, if desired. Serve with crackers, toast rounds, or crisp vegetables.

SOUPER DUPER SANDWICHES

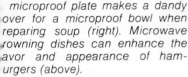

microproof plate makes a dandy over for a microproof bowl when reparing soup (right). Microwave rowning dishes can enhance the avor and appearance of hamurgers (above).

Yes, indeed, soup is super when prepared in the microwave oven! You can prepare canned or instant soup right in the serving bowl or mug. But don't you agree that nothing is more reassuring than a steaming bowl of your very own homemade soup? Now, you'll prepare your own more often. Imagine the convenience of cooking in the serving tureen (any nice and large casserole will do) and then ladling leftover soup from the refrigerator container into a mug for reheating and serving. No pan to clean!

Sandwiches, too, are so easy and most can be prepared simply wrapped in waxed paper or paper towels.

Best of all, of course, are the marvelous soup and sandwich combinations you can serve for lunch, brunch, or a quick dinner. Here are two of our selections: Manhattan Seafood Chowder (page 52) with Tuna, Tomato and Cheese (page 60). Quick Minestrone (page 51) with Ranch Burgers (page 59).

Converting Your Recipes

An enormous variety of sandwich combinations can be made in your microwave oven. Sandwiches heat quickly, so be careful not to overcook — the bread can become tough and chewy. Heat breads until warm, not hot, and cheese just until it begins to melt. Follow these tips when adapting or creating your own sandwiches:

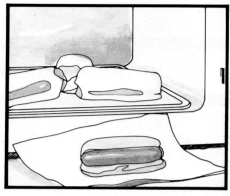

Arrange hot dogs and similar sandwiches like the spokes of a wheel.

☐ The best breads to use for warmed sandwiches are day-old, full-bodied breads such as rye and whole wheat, and breads rich in eggs and shortening, like French or Italian.

☐ Heat sandwiches on paper napkins, paper towels, or paper plates to absorb the steam and prevent sogginess. To prevent splattering, you can wrap each sandwich in a paper towel. Remove wrapping immediately after warming. It takes less than 1 minute to heat most sandwiches. (Cook on HI (max. power).)

☐ Thin slices of meat heat more quickly and taste better than one thick slice. The slower-cooking thick slice often causes bread to overcook before meat is hot.

☐ Moist fillings, such as that in a Sloppy Joe or a barbecued beef sandwich, should generally be heated separately from the rolls, to prevent sogginess.

☐ The browning dish can be used to enhance your grilled cheese or Reuben. Brown the buttered outer side of bread before inserting filling.

Soup converts well and easily to the microwave method. Find a recipe here with the approximate density and volume of the family favorite or the new conventional recipe you want to try. You may have to alter an ingredient or two: for example, dried bean soups, such as split pea and navy bean, do not obtain the best results in microwave cooking. However, canned, precooked beans and packaged dry soup mixes are perfect substitutes. The following tips will help you obtain excellent results with your own recipes:

☐ Be careful with milk-based liquids or large quantities, which can boil over quickly. Always select a large enough microproof container to prevent any boiling over, and fill individual cups no more than two-thirds full.

☐ Soup is cooked covered. Use microproof casserole lids, waxed paper, or plastic wrap.

☐ Cooking time varies with the volume of liquid and density of food in soup.

☐ Remember that the microwave's brief cooking time results in less evaporation of liquid than stovetop simmering.

☐ Start with one-quarter the time recommended in a conventional recipe and adjust as needed to complete cooking.

☐ The temperature of the liquid before heating will make a difference in final heating time. Water cold from the tap or drinks from the refrigerator will take somewhat longer than hot tap water or any room temperature liquid.

☐ You can use a microwave food thermometer to check the temperature of soup. Most people prefer 150°F for soup.

COOKING GUIDE — CANNED SOUPS

Soup	Amount	Power Control Setting	Time (minutes)	Special Notes
Broth	10¾ oz.	HI (max. power)	5 - 6½	Use 1½-quart casserole.
Cream-style	10¾ oz.	HI (max. power)	6 - 8	Use 1½-quart casserole.
Tomato	26 oz.	HI (max. power)	15 - 17	Use 2-quart casserole.
Bean, pea, or mushroom	10¾ oz.	HI (max. power)	6 - 8	Use 1½-quart casserole.
Undiluted chunk-style vegetable:	10¾ oz.	HI (max. power)	3 - 4½	Use 1-quart casserole.
	19 oz.	HI (max. power)	5½ - 7½	Use 1½-quart casserole.

● Add milk or water as directed on can. Stir.
● Stir cream-style soup halfway through cooking time.
● Let stand, covered, 3 minutes before serving.

COOKING GUIDE — QUICK SOUPS

Soup	Number of Envelopes	Power Control Setting	Time (minutes)	Special Notes
Instant soup 1¼-ounce envelope	1	HI (max. power)	2 - 3	Use ⅔ cup water in 8-ounce mug.
	2	HI (max. power)	3½ - 4½	Use ⅔ cup water per 8-ounce mug.
	4	HI (max. power)	7½ - 9	Use ⅔ cup water per 8-ounce mug.
Soup mix 2¾-ounce envelope	1	HI (max. power)	10 - 12½	Use 4 cups water in 2-quart casserole.

Eldorado Chili _____ 4 servings

Total Cooking Time: 33 to 38 minutes

1 pound lean ground beef
½ cup minced onion
½ cup chopped green pepper
1 clove garlic, minced
1 can (28 ounces) tomatoes, broken up, liquid reserved
1 can (15 ounces) kidney beans, undrained
½ cup broken spaghetti
1½ to 2 tablespoons chili powder
½ teaspoon cumin
½ teaspoon salt

Place ground beef in 2-quart microproof casserole; break up with fork. Add onion, green pepper, and garlic. Cover. Cook on HI (max. power) 7 to 8 minutes, stirring once during cooking time. Break up ground beef with fork; drain. Add remaining ingredients; mix lightly. Cover. Cook on HI (max. power) 26 to 30 minutes, or until spaghetti is cooked, stirring every 10 minutes during cooking time. Let stand 10 minutes before serving.

Seafood Corn Chowder _____ 4 to 6 servings

Total Cooking Time: 22 to 26 minutes

4 slices bacon, diced
½ cup chopped onion
1 tablespoon minced green pepper
1 can (16 ounces) cream-style corn
1 can (10¾ ounces) cream of potato soup
1 can (7½ ounces) minced clams, undrained
1 can (4½ ounces) small shrimp, drained
1½ cups milk
¼ teaspoon white pepper
1 tablespoon parsley flakes

Place bacon in 2-quart microproof casserole. Cover with paper towels. Cook on HI (max. power) 5 to 6 minutes, or until crisp. Remove bacon with slotted spoon; set aside. Drain all but 1 tablespoon bacon drippings from casserole. Add onion and green pepper. Cover. Cook on HI (max. power) 5 minutes, or until onion is transparent. Stir in corn, potato soup, clams, shrimp, milk, pepper, and parsley. Cover. Cook on HI (max. power) 12 to 15 minutes, or until hot, stirring twice during cooking time. Sprinkle bacon pieces on individual servings. Serve hot.

Split Pea and Ham Soup _____ 6 servings

Total Cooking Time: 65 minutes

5 cups water
1 smoked ham hock
   (½ pound)
1 cup chopped onion
1 package (6 ounces) split
   pea soup mix
3 black peppercorns
1 clove garlic, minced
1 bay leaf
½ teaspoon salt
½ teaspoon white pepper

Combine all ingredients in shallow 3-quart microproof bowl. Cover with plastic wrap. Cook on HI (max. power) 60 minutes, or until peas are tender. Remove ham hock from soup; cool until ham hock can be handled and meat cut from bone. Add meat to soup. Discard peppercorns and bay leaf. Add 1 cup water. Stir. Cook on HI (max. power) 5 minutes, or until heated through.

Hearty Tomato Soup _____ 6 servings

Total Cooking Time: 30 to 32 minutes

2 medium onions, chopped
3 tablespoons butter or
   margarine
1 can (28 ounces) tomatoes,
   broken up, liquid
   reserved
3 cups beef broth or
   bouillon
½ teaspoon salt
¼ teaspoon oregano
¼ teaspoon freshly ground
   pepper
   Shredded Cheddar cheese

Combine onions and butter in 2-quart microproof casserole. Cook on HI (max. power) 13 to 15 minutes, or until onions are transparent, stirring once during cooking time. Add remaining ingredients, except cheese; stir. Cover. Cook on HI (max. power) 17 minutes, or until heated through. Let stand 10 minutes. Purée in container of electric blender or food processor. Serve in bowls sprinkled with Cheddar cheese.

If you'd like to cut about 300 calories from this recipe, substitute 3 tablespoons beef broth or bouillon for butter when cooking the onions.

Turkey Soup _____ 6 servings

Total Cooking Time: 74 minutes

¾ pound turkey wings
5 cups water
1 cup chopped onions
½ cup thinly sliced carrots
½ cup thinly sliced celery
1 bay leaf
2½ teaspoons salt
⅛ teaspoon freshly ground
   pepper
1 tablespoon instant
   chicken bouillon

Combine all ingredients except bouillon in shallow 3-quart microproof bowl. Cover. Cook on HI (max. power) 39 minutes, or until mixture is boiling. Rearrange turkey. Cook on 75 (simmer) 30 minutes, or until turkey is tender. Add more water if necessary, to keep turkey covered. Remove turkey from broth with slotted spoon. Let stand until cool enough to handle; remove and discard bone and skin. Cut meat into bite-size pieces; return to broth. Discard bay leaf. Stir in bouillon. Cook on HI (max. power) 5 minutes, or until heated through. Serve immediately.

Tuna-Vegetable Soup _____ 3 to 4 servings

Total Cooking Time: 37 to 39 minutes

2 cups water
1 medium potato, peeled and
   sliced
¼ cup chopped onion
¼ cup diced carrot
¼ cup sliced celery
1 teaspoon chopped chives
1 teaspoon Worcestershire
   sauce
½ teaspoon salt
3 cubes chicken bouillon
   Dash freshly ground
   pepper
¾ cup fresh or frozen corn,
   (thaw, if frozen)
1 can (7 ounces) tuna,
   drained and flaked
1 cup light cream or
   half-and-half

In 2-quart microproof casserole, combine water, potato, onion, carrot, celery, chives, Worcestershire, salt, bouillon, and pepper. Cover. Cook on HI (max. power) 17 minutes, or until all vegetables are tender. Add corn. Cover. Cook on HI (max. power) 17 minutes, or until corn is tender. Stir in tuna and cream. Cover. Cook on HI (max. power) 3 to 5 minutes, or until heated through. Stir; let stand 5 minutes before serving.

_____

To reduce calories, substitute 1 cup evaporated low-fat milk for 1 cup light cream.

Corn and Sausage Chowder _____ 6 servings

Total Cooking Time: 27½ to 31½ minutes

½ pound link pork sausage
1 small onion, chopped
¼ cup chopped green pepper
1 can (17 ounces)
    cream-style corn
1½ cups milk
1 can (10¾ ounces)
    condensed cream of
    potato soup
3 teaspoons chopped pimiento
1 teaspoon salt
¼ teaspoon freshly ground
pepper

Place sausage in 2-quart microproof casserole; cover with paper towels. Cook on HI (max. power) 7 to 9 minutes, or until no longer pink, rearranging once during cooking time. Remove sausages from casserole; set aside to cool, reserving 1 tablespoon drippings in casserole. Add onion and green pepper to drippings. Cook on HI (max. power) 2½ minutes, or until onion is transparent. Slice sausages. Add sausages and remaining ingredients; stir to blend. Cover. Cook on HI (max. power) 18 to 20 minutes, or until mixture boils, stirring once during cooking.

Quick Minestrone _____ 6 servings

Total Cooking Time: 41 to 43 minutes

1 cup cubed cooked beef or
    ham
1 can (16 ounces) tomatoes,
    broken up
1 can (15 ounces) kidney
    beans, undrained
1 can (10¾ ounces)
    condensed tomato soup
1 cup water
½ cup shredded cabbage
⅓ cup uncooked vermicelli,
    broken in 1-inch pieces
1 clove garlic, minced
1 tablespoon Worcestershire
    sauce
½ teaspoon salt
½ teaspoon basil
¼ teaspoon freshly ground
    pepper
    Grated Parmesan cheese

Combine all ingredients, except Parmesan cheese, in shallow 3-quart microproof bowl. Cover with plastic wrap. Cook on HI (max. power) 41 to 43 minutes, or until vermicelli is cooked, stirring twice during cooking time. Let stand 10 minutes. Serve in bowls sprinkled with Parmesan cheese.

Manhattan Seafood Chowder ___ 5 to 6 servings
Total Cooking Time: 23 to 25 minutes

1 package (16 ounces) frozen
 cod, flounder, or
 haddock fillets
2 tablespoons vegetable oil
1 medium green pepper,
 seeded and cut in
 thin strips
1 small onion, sliced
1 clove garlic, minced
1 can (16 ounces) tomatoes
1 bottle (8 ounces) clam juice
1/4 teaspoon basil
1/4 teaspoon salt
1/8 teaspoon white pepper
1 can (10 ounces) minced clams,
 undrained

Partially thaw frozen fish per instructions (page 131). Cut into chunks and set aside. In shallow 3-quart microproof bowl, combine oil, green pepper, onion, and garlic. Cook on HI (max. power) 5 minutes, stirring once. Add fish, tomatoes, clam juice, basil, salt, and pepper. Cook on HI (max. power) 15 minutes. Add clams and liquid; stir. Cook on HI (max. power) 3 to 5 minutes, or until heated through and fish flakes easily.

Onion-Beef Soup _____ 4 servings
Total Cooking Time: 18 to 21 minutes

2 medium onions, thinly
 sliced
1/4 cup butter or margarine
3 cups beef broth
1 teaspoon Worcestershire
 sauce
1 teaspoon salt
1 teaspoon soy sauce
1/2 teaspoon paprika
 Grated Parmesan cheese

Combine onions and butter in 2-quart microproof casserole. Cover. Cook on HI (max. power) 9 to 10 minutes, or until onions are transparent, stirring once during cooking time. Stir in remaining ingredients, except cheese. Cook on HI (max. power) 9 to 11 minutes, or until hot. Serve in bowls with cheese sprinkled on top.

Manhattan Seafood Chowder→

Beef Vegetable Soup ———————— 4 servings
Total Cooking Time: 32 to 37 minutes

½ pound lean ground beef
2½ cups water
1 can (8 ounces) tomatoes, broken up, liquid reserved
1 package (10 ounces) frozen mixed vegetables, thawed
½ cup uncooked noodles
1 envelope onion soup mix
1 bay leaf
⅛ teaspoon freshly ground pepper

Place ground beef in 2-quart microproof casserole; break up with fork. Cook on HI (max. power) 6 to 7 minutes, or until beef is no longer red, stirring once during cooking. Break up ground beef with fork; drain. Stir in remaining ingredients. Cover. Cook on HI (max. power) 26 to 30 minutes, or until mixture boils and noodles are cooked, stirring every 10 minutes. Let stand, covered, 10 minutes. Discard bay leaf before serving.

Lemon Chicken Rice Soup ————— 4 servings
Total Cooking Time: 28 minutes

4 cups chicken broth
¼ cup instant rice
3 eggs
3 tablespoons lemon juice
1 cup minced cooked chicken

Pour broth into 2-quart glass bowl. Cook on HI (max. power) 22 minutes. Add rice. Cover and let stand 5 minutes. Beat eggs until foamy. Beat in lemon juice. Gradually add 1 cup hot broth to egg mixture, beating constantly. Stir egg mixture into remaining hot broth. Cook on HI (max. power) 5 minutes, or until soup is thickened, stirring every 2 minutes. Stir in chicken. Cook on HI (max. power) 1 minute. Serve in bowls garnished with a lemon slice, if desired.

Hot Dog Cheese Wrap _____ 2 servings

Total Cooking Time: 3½ to 4 minutes

2 slices bacon
2 hot dog buns
1 tablespoon mustard
1 slice Cheddar cheese
2 hot dogs

Place bacon between 2 sheets of paper towels. Cook on HI (max. power) 2 minutes, or until partially cooked. Split buns; spread with mustard; set aside. Cut cheese into 8 ¼-inch strips; divide cheese into 2 stacks. Cut each hot dog lengthwise in half, almost through. Lay cheese strips in slit. Wrap bacon strip around each hot dog. Place hot dogs in buns. Wrap each with paper towels or napkin. Cook on HI (max. power) 1½ to 2 minutes. Let stand 1 minute before serving.

Any favorite cheese can be substituted for Cheddar cheese.

Beef Tacos and Fixin's _____ 8 servings

Total Cooking Time: 9½ minutes

1 pound lean ground beef
½ cup chopped onion
1 clove garlic, minced
½ cup tomato juice
1 package (1¼ ounces) taco seasoning mix
8 taco shells
2 cups shredded lettuce
2 medium tomatoes, chopped
1½ cups shredded Cheddar cheese
1 medium onion, finely chopped
1 avocado, diced

Place beef in 2-quart microproof casserole; break up with fork. Add onion and garlic. Cook on HI (max. power) 5 minutes, or until beef is no longer red, stirring several times during cooking time; drain. Stir in juice and taco seasoning. Cook on HI (max. power) 3½ minutes, or until heated through. Arrange taco shells on microproof plate. Cook on HI (max. power) 1 minute. Divide beef mixture, lettuce, tomatoes, cheese, onion, and avocado among shells. Serve with a favorite hot sauce, if desired.

Triple Decker Favorite _____ 1 serving

Total Cooking Time: 2 minutes

Butter or margarine
2 slices white bread, toasted
1 slice chicken
  Salt
  Freshly ground pepper
1 slice bacon, cooked until
    crisp (Guide, page 101)
  Mayonnaise
1 slice whole wheat bread,
    toasted
  Mustard
1 slice Swiss cheese
1 medium tomato, sliced

Butter white toast on 1 side. Place chicken on 1 slice toast; sprinkle with salt and pepper. Break bacon in half and place on chicken. Spread mayonnaise on 1 side of whole wheat toast. Place whole wheat toast, mayonnaise-side down, on top of bacon. Spread top of whole wheat toast with mustard. Add Swiss cheese and tomato slices. Sprinkle with salt and pepper. Top with remaining toast, buttered side down. Wrap sandwich in paper napkin and place on microproof plate. Cook on 60 (braise) 2 minutes, or until cheese is melted and sandwich is warm. Cut in half to serve.

Two sandwiches can be cooked at the same time. Double cooking time.

Barbecued Beef _____ 2 servings

Total Cooking Time: 2 to 3 minutes

1 cup shredded cooked
    roast beef
3 tablespoons catsup
½ envelope onion soup mix
  Dash Worcestershire sauce
2 hamburger buns, split

Combine all ingredients, except buns, in 1½-quart microproof casserole. Cover. Cook on HI (max. power) 1½ to 2 minutes, or until heated through, stirring once during cooking time. Spoon mixture onto bottoms of buns; cover with tops. Place on paper towel-lined microproof plate. Cook on 50 (defrost) 30 to 60 seconds, or until buns are warm.

Lemon Chicken Rice Soup (page 54), Triple Decker Favorite →

Super Sandwich _____ 1 serving

Total Cooking Time: 2½ to 3½ minutes

1 slice (1-inch thick)
    Italian bread or 1
    large hard roll, split
1 tablespoon butter or
    margarine
1 slice bologna
1 slice summer sausage
⅓ cup sauerkraut, drained
1 slice mozzarella cheese
    Paprika

Spread bread with butter. Cut bologna and sausage in half. Place meat slices alternately on bread. Top with sauerkraut. Sprinkle with cheese. Place sandwich on paper towel-lined microproof plate. Cook on 50 (defrost) 2½ to 3½ minutes, or until cheese is melted and sandwich is heated through. Sprinkle with paprika. Let stand 1 minute before serving.

To heat 4 sandwiches, arrange in circle on plate. Cook on 50 (defrost) 10 to 12 minutes.

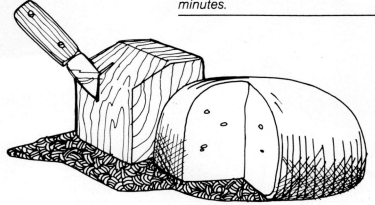

Hoboburgers _____ 8 servings

Total Cooking Time: 12 minutes

1 pound lean ground beef
½ cup chopped onion
¼ cup chopped green pepper
1 can (6 ounces) tomato
    paste
1 can (15 ounces) kidney
    beans, drained
1 teaspoon salt
⅛ teaspoon freshly ground
    pepper
8 hamburger buns, toasted

Combine beef, onion, and green pepper in 2-quart microproof casserole. Cook on HI (max. power) 5 minutes, or until beef is no longer red, stirring once during cooking time. Break up beef with fork; drain. Add remaining ingredients, except buns. Blend well. Cover. Cook on HI (max. power) 7 minutes, stirring twice during cooking time. Spoon onto bottoms of hamburger buns; cover with tops.

Cheeseburger _____ 4 servings

Total Cooking Time: 6 to 7½ minutes

1 pound lean ground beef
 Garlic salt
 Freshly ground pepper
4 hamburger buns, split and
 toasted
4 slices process American
 cheese

Season ground beef with garlic salt and pepper. Shape into 4 patties. Arrange in 10-inch round microproof baking dish. Cover with waxed paper. Cook on HI (max. power) 2½ minutes. Turn patties over; season. Cover. Cook on HI (max. power) 2½ to 3½ minutes, or until desired degree of doneness.

Place patties on bottoms of hamburger buns. Top each with slice of cheese. Place cheeseburgers in a circle on 10-inch paper towel-lined microproof plate. Cook on HI (max. power) 1 to 1½ minutes, or until cheese is melted. Cover with tops of buns. Let stand 1 minute before serving.

Ranchburgers _____ 4 servings

Total Cooking Time: 11 to 12 minutes

1 cup sauerkraut, drained
½ cup cranberry sauce
¼ cup chili sauce or catsup
1 tablespoon brown sugar
1 pound lean ground beef
½ envelope onion soup mix
4 onion rolls, split

Combine sauerkraut, cranberry sauce, chili sauce, and brown sugar in 1-quart microproof casserole; mix well. Cook on HI (max. power) 5 minutes, stirring once during cooking time. Cover and set aside.

Combine ground beef and soup mix; blend thoroughly. Shape into 4 patties. Arrange in 10-inch round microproof baking dish. Cover with waxed paper. Cook on HI (max. power) 3 minutes. Turn patties over; cover. Cook on HI (max. power) 3 to 4 minutes, or until desired degree of doneness.

Place patties on bottoms of rolls. Top with hot sauerkraut mixture. Cover with tops of rolls.

Tuna, Tomato, and Cheese _____ 6 servings

Total Cooking Time: 2 to 3½ minutes

3 English muffins, split
   and toasted
3 tablespoons butter or
   margarine
1 large tomato, cut in
   6 slices
1 can (6½ ounces) tuna,
   drained and flaked
2 tablespoons mayonnaise
3 slices Cheddar or Swiss
   cheese

Spread muffins with butter. Arrange in circle on large paper towel-lined microproof plate. Place tomato slice on each muffin. Mix tuna and mayonnaise until blended. Divide and spoon tuna over tomato slices. Cut cheese diagonally in half to form triangles. Place 1 triangle of cheese on each muffin. Cook on HI (max. power) 2 to 3½ minutes, or until cheese is melted and muffin topping is warm. Let stand 2 minutes before serving.

A single split muffin can be prepared and cooked on HI (max. power) cycle for 40 to 60 seconds. Toasted bread can be substituted for English muffins.

Mushrooms Benedict _____ 4 servings

Total Cooking Time: 5½ to 6½ minutes

1 cup (4 ounces) sliced
   mushrooms
1 tablespoon butter or
   margarine
⅓ cup water
3 teaspoons all-purpose
   flour
½ teaspoon instant beef
   bouillon granules
½ teaspoon Worcestershire
   sauce
¼ cup dairy sour cream
1 teaspoon parsley flakes
2 English muffins, split
   and toasted
4 slices cooked ham

In 2-cup glass measure, combine mushrooms and butter. Cook on HI (max. power) 2 to 2½ minutes, or until tender, stirring once during cooking time. Use slotted spoon to remove mushrooms; set aside; reserve liquid. In small microproof bowl, blend water, flour, bouillon, and Worcestershire; stir into mushroom liquid. Cook on HI (max. power) 1½ to 2 minutes, or until thickened, stirring once during cooking time. Stir in sour cream, parsley, and mushrooms.

Place muffins on paper towel-lined microproof plate. Place a slice of ham on each muffin half. Cook on 50 (defrost) 2 minutes, or until ham is heated through. Remove to serving plate. Top each with ¼ cup mushroom sauce. Serve immediately.

A LA CARTE

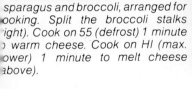

...sparagus and broccoli, arranged for ...ooking. Split the broccoli stalks ...ight). Cook on 55 (defrost) 1 minute ...o warm cheese. Cook on HI (max. ...ower) 1 minute to melt cheese ...above).

Here's where you'll find all the special side dishes that help make a banquet out of any entrée. You'll also discover the microwave way for "special order" and traditional egg or cheese dishes.

Vegetables and the microwave oven were made for each other, or so you'll think when you sit down with one of these dishes on the table. Just think — little water, and sometimes none at all, is used in cooking vegetables. They don't lose any vitamins and keep just-picked flavor and color.

Potatoes? You bet. There's no more dramatic example of microwave cooking speed than a baked potato that took all of 6 to 8 minutes to cook!

But, let's face it, nothing is absolutely perfect. Pasta and rice cook fine in the microwave but no time is saved. That's because they must be reconstituted and there's no way to shorten the conventional timing. They do reheat incredibly well, however.

Converting Your Recipes

As you convert, consider that vegetables are at their best when served crisp-tender, as in wok cooking. For a softer texture, however, simply add a bit more water and increase cooking time until they reach the texture you prefer. All vegetables use HI (max. power). To convert that family favorite, simply find a similar recipe here or look for timing hints in the Guides.

- ☐ You can use a microwave food thermometer when cooking most vegetable dishes. 150°F is the usually preferred temperature for doneness.
- ☐ Pasta, rice, and cereals are best when added to other ingredients, as in vegetable, meat, or cheese casseroles. While the oven can cook them separately, there's no advantage. It is wise to reheat them in the oven, however. You add no water and they are like fresh cooked. Cook on HI (max. power) 4 to 5 minutes for 1 cup (cooked), 6 to 7 minutes for 2 cups, etc. Cover tightly.
- ☐ Grits or other hot cereals are interesting side dishes for brunch, cooked in individual bowls. Cook on HI (max. power) 8 to 9 minutes for $\frac{1}{3}$ cup grits (uncooked); 2 to 3 minutes for $\frac{1}{3}$ cup quick oatmeal. Follow package directions for liquid.
- ☐ To reheat mashed potatoes, cook on HI (max. power) 3 to $3\frac{1}{2}$ minutes.
- ☐ Eggs are undercooked slightly and allowed to complete cooking during standing time. Eggs are cooked covered to trap steam and assure even cooking.

Cut carrots diagonally to expose more area for faster cooking. It's also a bit more attractive. Cut all vegetables uniformally when possible.

COOKING GUIDE — SCRAMBLED EGGS
Cook on 90 (bake).

Number of Eggs	Liquid (Milk or Cream)	Butter	Minutes to Cook
1	1 tablespoon	1 teaspoon	1 - 1½
2	2 tablespoons	2 teaspoons	2 - 3
4	3 tablespoons	3 teaspoons	3½ - 4½
6	4 tablespoons	4 teaspoons	6 - 7

● Break eggs into a microproof bowl or glass measure. Add milk or cream. Beat with a fork. Add butter. Cover with waxed paper. Stir at least once during cooking time from the outside to the center. Let stand 1 minute before serving.

COOKING GUIDE — POACHED EGGS
Cook on HI (max. power).

Number of Eggs	Water	Container	Minutes to Boil Water	Minutes to Cook
1	¼ cup	6-ounce microproof custard cup	1½ - 2½	1
2	¼ cup	6-ounce microproof custard cups	2 - 3	1½-2
3	¼ cup	6-ounce microproof custard cups	3½ to 4½	3-3½
4	1 cup	1-quart microproof dish	5 - 6	4-5

● Bring water to a boil with a pinch of salt and up to ¼ teaspoon vinegar. Break egg carefully into hot water. Pierce egg lightly with toothpick. Cover with waxed paper. Let stand, covered, 1 minute before serving.

COOKING GUIDE — RICE

Food	Amount Uncooked	Water	Minutes to Full Boil HI (max. power)	Power Control Setting	Time (minutes)	Standing Time (minutes)	Special Notes
Short-grain	1 cup	2 cups	6 - 6½	75 (simmer)	13 - 15	5	2-quart casserole.
Long-grain	1 cup	2 cups	6 - 6½	75 (simmer)	15 - 17	5	2-quart casserole.
Wild rice	1 cup	3 cups	9 - 10	75 (simmer)	35 - 40	5	3-quart casserole.
Brown rice	1 cup	3 cups	9 - 10	75 (simmer)	40	5	3-quart casserole.
Quick-cooking	1 cup	1 cup	3½ - 4	HI (max. power)	0	5	1-quart casserole.

● Add salt and butter or margarine according to package directions. Cover tightly. Let stand, covered, 5 minutes before serving.

Vegetable Cooking Tips

1. Choose a wide, shallow dish so vegetables can be spread out.
2. Cover all vegetables tightly.
3. Pouches of frozen vegetables require steam vents. Slit pouch and cook on microproof dish.
4. Frozen vegetables without sauces can be cooked in their cartons without water. Remove waxed paper wrapping before placing carton in oven. (Remove frozen-in-sauce vegetables if they are packaged in cartons rather than pouches. Place in 1½-quart microproof casserole. Add liquid before cooking according to package directions.)
5. Vegetables packaged in foil should be removed from package and placed in microproof dish.
6. After cooking, allow all vegetables to stand, covered, 2 to 3 minutes.

COOKING GUIDE — VEGETABLES

Cook on HI (max. power).

Food	Amount	Vegetable Preparation	Time (minutes)	Water	Special Notes
Artichokes 3½″ in diameter ½ lb. (med.)	Fresh: 1	Wash thoroughly. Cut tops off each leaf.	8 - 10	¼ cup	When done, a leaf peeled from whole comes off easily.
	2		12 - 14	½ cup	
	Frozen: 10 oz.	Slit pouch.	6 - 7½		
Asparagus: spears and cut pieces	Fresh: 1 lb.	Wash thoroughly. Snap off tough base and discard.	4½ - 5½	¼ cup	Stir or rearrange once during cooking time.
	Frozen: 10 oz.		8 - 10	None	
Beans: green, wax, French-cut	Fresh: 1 lb.	Remove ends. Wash well. Leave whole or break in pieces.	12 - 14	¼ cup	Stir once or rearrange as necessary.
	Frozen: 6 oz.		6 - 8½	None	
Beets	4 medium	Scrub beets. Leave 1″ of top on beet.	18 - 21	¼ cup	After cooking, peel. Cut or leave whole.
Broccoli	Fresh, whole, 1-1½ lbs.	Remove outer leaves. Slit stalks.	13 - 15	¼ cup	Stir or rearrange during cooking time.
	Frozen, whole		12 - 14	¼ cup	
	Fresh, chopped, 1-1½ lbs.		11 - 12	¼ cup	
	Frozen, chopped, 10 oz.		10 - 12	None	
Brussels sprouts	Fresh: 1 lb.	Remove outside leaves if wilted. Cut off stems. Wash.	10 - 12	¼ cup	Stir or rearrange once during cooking time.
	Frozen: 10 oz.		8 - 10	None	
Cabbage	½ medium head, shredded	Remove outside wilted leaves.	7 - 9	¼ cup	
	1 medium head, wedges		16 - 18	¼ cup	Rearrange wedges after 7 minutes.

Food	Amount	Vegetable Preparation	Time (minutes)	Water	Special Notes
Carrots	4: sliced or diced	Peel and cut off tops.	8 - 10	1 Tb.	Stir once during cooking time.
	6: sliced or diced	Fresh young carrots cook best.	11 - 13	2 Tbs.	
	8 tiny, whole		11 - 13	2 Tbs.	
	Frozen: 10 oz.		9 - 11	None	
Cauliflower	1 medium, in florets	Cut tough stem. Wash, remove outside leaves.	10 - 12	¼ cup	Stir after 5 minutes.
	1 medium, whole	Remove core.	11 - 13	¼ cup	Turn over once.
	Frozen: 10 oz.		9 - 11	¼ cup	
Celery	2½ cups, 1″ slices	Clean stalks thoroughly.	9 - 11	¼ cup	Stir after 5 minutes.
Corn: kernel	Frozen: 10 oz.		6 - 8	¼ cup	Stir halfway through cooking time.
on the cob	1 ear	Husk, wrap each	5 - 6	None	Rearrange halfway
	2 ears	in waxed paper. Place	7 - 8	None	through cooking time
	3 ears	on glass tray in oven.	10 - 12	None	unless cooked on
	4 ears	Cook no more than 4 at a time.	13 - 15	None	microproof rack.
	Frozen,	Flat dish, covered.			
	2 ears		7 - 8½	None	Rearrange halfway
	4 ears		12 - 14	None	through cooking time.
Eggplant	1 medium, sliced	Wash and peel. Cut into slices or cubes.	6 - 8	2 Tbs.	
	1 medium, whole	Pierce skin.	7 - 9		Place on micro-proof rack.
Greens: collard, kale, etc.	Fresh: 1 lb.	Wash. Remove wilted leaves or tough stem.	8 - 10	None	
	Frozen: 10 oz.		8 - 10	None	
Mushrooms	Fresh: ½ lb., sliced	Add butter or water.	3 - 4	2 Tbs.	Stir halfway through cooking time.
Okra	Fresh: ½ lb.	Wash thoroughly. Leave whole or cut	4 - 6	¼ cup	
	Frozen: 10 oz.	in thick slices.	9 - 10	None	
Onions	1 lb., tiny whole	Peel. Add 1 Tb. butter.	8 - 10	¼ cup	Stir once during cooking time.
	1 lb., medium to large	Peel and quarter. Add 1 Tb. butter.	9 - 11	¼ cup	
Parsnips	4 medium, quartered	Peel and cut.	10 - 12	¼ cup	Stir once during cooking time.
Peas: green	Fresh: 1 lb.	Shell peas. Rinse well.	9 - 10	¼ cup	Stir once during cooking time.
	Fresh: 2 lbs.		12 - 13	½ cup	
	Frozen: 6 oz.		5 - 7	None	
Peas and onions	Frozen: 10 oz.		6½ - 8	2 Tbs.	
Pea pods	Frozen: 6 oz.		4 - 5	2 Tbs.	
Potatoes, sweet 5 - 6 oz. ea.	1	Scrub well. Pierce with fork. Place on rack or paper towel in circle, 1″ apart.	6 - 9	None	Rearrange halfway through cooking time.
	2		10 - 12	None	
	4		16 - 19	None	
	6		20 - 23	None	

Cooking Guide for Vegetables is continued on next page→

Food	Amount	Vegetable Preparation	Time (minutes)	Water	Special Notes
Potatoes, white baking 6 - 8 oz. ea.	1 2 3 4 5	Wash and scrub well. Pierce with fork. Place on rack or paper towel in circle, 1″ apart.	7 - 9 13 - 15 17 - 19 23 - 25 27 - 29	None None None None None	Rearrange halfway through cooking time.
russet, boiling	3	Peel potatoes, cut in quarters.	13 - 16	½ cup	Stir once during cooking time.
Rutabaga	Fresh: 1 lb. Frozen: 10 oz.	Wash well. Remove tough stems or any wilted leaves.	7 - 9 8 - 10	None None	Stir once during cooking time.
Spinach	Fresh: 1 lb. Frozen: 10 oz.	Wash well. Remove tough stems. Drain.	7 - 8 8 - 10	None None	Stir once during cooking time.
Squash, acorn or butternut	1 - 1½ lbs. whole	Scrub. Pierce with fork.	13 - 16		Cut and remove seeds to serve.
Spaghetti squash	2 - 3 lbs.	Scrub, pierce. Place on rack.	8 per lb.	None	Serve with butter, Parmesan cheese, spaghetti sauce. Let stand 5 minutes.
Turnips	4 cups, cubed	Peel, wash.	12 - 15	¼ cup	Stir after 5 minutes.
Zucchini	3 cups, sliced	Wash; do not peel.	5 - 7	¼ cup	Stir after 4 minutes.

COOKING GUIDE — CONVENIENCE VEGETABLES

Food	Amount	Power Control Setting	Time (minutes)	Special Notes
Au gratin vegetables, frozen	11½ oz.	HI (max. power)	10 - 12	Use glass loaf dish, covered.
Baked beans, frozen	6 oz.	HI (max. power)	8 - 11	Use 1½-quart casserole, covered. Stir once.
Corn, scalloped frozen	12 oz.	HI (max. power)	7 - 9	Use 1-quart casserole, covered.
Potatoes, stuffed, frozen	2	HI (max. power)	10 - 12	Use shallow dish. Cover with waxed paper.
Tots, frozen	16 oz. 32 oz.	HI (max. power)	9 - 12 13 - 17	Use 2-quart round or oval baking dish. Rearrange once.
Creamed potato mix	4 - 5 oz.	HI (max. power)	25 - 30	
Au gratin, frozen	11½ oz.	HI (max. power)	15 - 20	Use 1½-quart casserole, covered with waxed paper.
Instant mashed	3½ oz. packet	HI (max. power)	8 - 10	Use covered casserole. Follow package directions. Reduce liquid by 1 tablespoon.
Peas, pea pods, chestnuts, frozen	10 oz.	HI (max. power)	10	Place pouch on plate. Slit pouch. Flex once during cooking time to mix.
Stuffing mix	6 oz.	HI (max. power)	12 - 14	Use 1½-quart casserole, covered. Follow package directions.

COOKING GUIDE — CANNED VEGETABLES
Cook on HI (max. power).

Size	Minutes Drained	Minutes Undrained	*Special Notes*
8 ounces 15 ounces 17 ounces	2 - 2½ 3 - 3½ 4 - 5	2 - 3 3 - 5 4½ - 6	Regardless of quantity: use a 4-cup microproof casserole, covered. Stir once. Let stand, covered, 2 - 3 minutes before serving.

The Blanching Guide

The microwave oven can be a valuable and appreciated aid in preparing fresh vegetables for the freezer. (The oven is, however, *not* recommended for canning.) Here are some tips in preparing vegetables for blanching:

☐ Measure amounts to be blanched; place by batches, in microproof casserole.
☐ Cover and cook on HI (max. power) for time indicated on chart.
☐ Stir vegetables halfway through cooking time.
☐ Let vegetables stand, covered, 1 minute after cooking.
☐ Place vegetables in ice water at once to stop cooking. When vegetables feel cool, spread on towel to absorb excess moisture.
☐ Package in freezer containers or pouches. Seal, label, date, and freeze.

BLANCHING GUIDE — VEGETABLES
Cook on HI (max. power).

Food	Amount	Water	Approximate Time (minutes)	Casserole Size
Asparagus (cut in 1-inch pieces)	4 cups	¼ cup	8	1½ quart
Beans, green or wax (cut in 1-inch pieces)	1 pound	½ cup	7-8	1½ quart
Broccoli (cut in 1-inch pieces)	1 pound	⅓ cup	8	1½ quart
Carrots (sliced)	1 pound	⅓ cup	8	1½ quart
Cauliflower (cut in florets)	1 head	⅓ cup	8	2 quart
Corn (cut from cob)	4 cups	none	5½	1½ quart
Corn-on-the-cob (husked)	6 ears	none	7	1½ quart
Onion (quartered)	4 medium	½ cup	4-6	1 quart
Parsnips (cubed)	1 pound	¼ cup	3½-5½	1½ quart
Peas (shelled)	4 cups	¼ cup	10	1½ quart
Snow peas	4 cups	¼ cup	4½-5	1½ quart
Spinach (washed)	1 pound	none	5½	2 quart
Turnips (cubed)	1 pound	¼ cup	4-6	1½ quart
Zucchini (sliced or cubed)	1 pound	¼ cup	5½	1½ quart

Acorn Squash with Peas ———————— 4 servings

Total Cooking Time: 33½ to 41½ minutes

2 acorn squash (1 to 1½ pounds each)
1 package (10 ounces) frozen peas
Salt
Freshly ground pepper
1 jar (4 ounces) pimiento, drained
1 tablespoon butter or margarine

Cook acorn squash according to Guide (page 66). Place package of peas on microproof plate. Cook on HI (max. power) 6 to 8 minutes, or until thawed and warm. While peas are thawing, cut squash in half lengthwise; scoop out seeds. Place cut-side up on microproof plate. Sprinkle each half with salt and pepper. In small dish, mix peas, pimiento, and butter. Divide among squash halves. Cook on HI (max. power) 1½ minutes. Serve hot.

Spinach with Cheese ———————— 6 to 8 servings

Total Cooking Time: 28½ to 33 minutes

1 package (10 ounces) frozen chopped spinach
1 cup White Sauce (page 73)
¼ teaspoon onion salt
⅛ teaspoon freshly ground pepper
2 large eggs, separated
3 slices Cheddar cheese, cut diagonally in half

Place unopened package of spinach on microproof plate. Cook on HI (max. power) 8 minutes; drain. Squeeze all moisture from spinach.

Prepare White Sauce in 2-quart glass bowl. Stir in spinach, salt, and pepper; set aside.

In mixing bowl, beat egg whites until stiff, but not dry; set aside. In another mixing bowl, beat egg yolks. Add yolks to spinach mixture; stir gently to blend. Carefully fold in egg whites. Pour into 9-inch round microproof dish. Smooth top with spatula. Cook on 50 (defrost) 12 to 16 minutes, or until center is set, rotating dish if cooking unevenly.

Arrange cheese triangles around outside of dish with points toward center. Cover with aluminum foil. Let stand 3 minutes to soften cheese.

Acorn Squash with Peas→

Carrot and Basil Bake _____ 6 servings
Total Cooking Time: 13 to 15½ minutes

1 pound carrots, peeled and
   shredded
1 small onion, minced
2 tablespoons butter or
   margarine
2 tablespoons water
1 teaspoon parsley flakes
½ teaspoon salt
½ teaspoon crushed sweet
   basil

Combine all ingredients in 1¾-quart microproof casserole. Cover. Cook on HI (max. power) 13 to 15½ minutes, stirring twice during cooking time. Let stand 3 minutes before serving.

String Beans and Pearl Onions ____ 7 servings
Total Cooking Time: 21 to 23 minutes

1 package (9 ounces) frozen
   whole green beans
1 package (10 ounces) frozen
   pearl onions in cream
   sauce, removed from pouch
⅛ teaspoon summer savory

Place green beans in 1¾-quart microproof casserole. Place onions in cream sauce over beans. Sprinkle with savory. Cook on 50 (defrost) 7 minutes, stirring once during cooking time. Cook on HI (max. power) 14 to 16 minutes, or until crisp-tender. Let stand 3 minutes before serving.

If you prefer, substitute 2 tablespoons pimiento for the onions. Reduce cooking time by 4 minutes.

Braised Celery and Peas _____ 6 servings
Total Cooking Time: 16 to 19 minutes

2 cups sliced celery, ¼
   inch thick
⅓ cup chopped onion
2 tablespoons butter or
   margarine
2 tablespoons water
½ teaspoon salt
¼ teaspoon celery salt
1 package (10 ounces)
   frozen peas
1 tablespoon minced fresh
   parsley

In 2-quart microproof casserole, combine celery, onion, butter, water, salt, and celery salt. Cover. Cook on HI (max. power) 9 to 10 minutes, or until vegetables are tender, stirring once during cooking time. Add peas. Cover. Cook on HI (max. power) 7 to 9 minutes, stirring after 4 minutes. Sprinkle with parsley before serving.

Garden Goodness ——————————— 6 servings

Total Cooking Time: 26 to 27 minutes

2 tablespoons butter or
  margarine
1 cup pearl onions,
  peeled
1 pound small new potatoes,
  washed
6 small carrots, peeled and
  cut into 1-inch pieces
⅓ cup water
1 tablespoon instant chicken
  bouillon granules
½ teaspoon salt
1 cup fresh or frozen peas
2 tablespoons minced parsley

Combine butter and onions in 2-quart microproof casserole. Cover. Cook on HI (max. power) 5 minutes. Add potatoes, carrots, water, bouillon, and salt. Cook on HI (max. power) 20 minutes, stirring once during cooking time. Add peas. Cover. Cook on HI (max. power) 1 to 2 minutes, or until vegetables are crisp-tender. Stir in parsley. Cover and let stand 5 minutes before serving.

Green Beans with Bacon ——————— 4 servings

Total Cooking Time: 23 to 24 minutes

2 slices bacon
⅓ cup chopped onion
1 pound fresh green beans,
  trimmed and cut in
  1-inch pieces

Cut bacon into small pieces; place in 2-quart microproof casserole. Add onion. Cover. Cook on HI (max. power) 8 minutes, or until bacon is brown and onion transparent. Add beans. Cover. Cook on HI (max. power) 15 to 16 minutes, or until beans are tender, stirring twice during cooking time. Let stand 3 minutes before serving.

Norwegian Red Cabbage ——————— 4 servings

Total Cooking Time: 29 minutes

1 small head (1 to 1½
  pounds) red cabbage,
  shredded
⅓ cup currant jelly
¼ cup water
3 tablespoons vinegar
2 tablespoons butter or
  margarine
½ teaspoon salt
¼ teaspoon caraway seeds

Place cabbage in 2-quart microproof casserole. Add remaining ingredients; stir lightly to mix. Cover. Cook on HI (max. power) 4 minutes. Stir carefully; cover. Cook on HI (max. power) 25 minutes, or until cabbage is tender, stirring twice during cooking time.

Asparagus with Mustard Sauce ____ 6 servings
Total Cooking Time: 7 to 9 minutes

1½ pounds asparagus, cleaned
    and cut in pieces
¼ cup water
⅓ cup mayonnaise
1 tablespoon minced fresh
    parsley
1 teaspoon prepared mustard
½ teaspoon onion salt
⅛ teaspoon white pepper

In 2-quart microproof casserole, combine asparagus and water. Cover. Cook on HI (max. power) 6 to 7 minutes, or until tender, stirring once during cooking time; drain. Combine remaining ingredients, mixing lightly to coat asparagus. Cook on HI (max. power) 1 to 2 minute, or until heated through.

Two packages (9 ounces each) frozen cut asparagus can be substituted for fresh asparagus; omit water.

Three Bean Bake _____ 8 to 10 servings
Total Cooking Time: 30 to 36 minutes

2 slices bacon, diced
1 small onion, chopped
1 can (31 ounces) pork and
    beans in tomato sauce
1 can (17 ounces) lima
    beans, drained
1 can (16 ounces) cut green
    beans, drained
¼ cup catsup
1 tablespoon prepared
    mustard

Place bacon in 2-quart microproof casserole. Cover. Cook on HI, (max. power) 5 to 6 minutes, or until crisp. Remove bacon; set aside, reserving drippings. Stir onion into drippings. Cover. Cook on HI, (max. power) 5 minutes, or until tender, stirring once during cooking time. Add remaining ingredients; stir. Cover. Cook on HI (max. power) 20 to 25 minutes, or until hot, stirring once. Top with reserved bacon and serve.

Corn-in-the-Husk _____ 4 servings
Total Cooking Time: 18 to 20 minutes

4 ears corn in husks
  Butter or margarine
  Salt
  Freshly ground pepper

Discard soiled outer portion of husk. Soak corn in cold water 10 minutes. Drain, but do not dry. Arrange corn on microproof plate. Cook on HI (max. power) 18 to 20 minutes, rearranging halfway through cooking time. Let stand 3 minutes. Peel and discard husks and silk. Serve with butter, salt, and pepper.

Broccoli and Sour Cream _____ 6 to 8 servings

Total Cooking Time: 18 to 20 minutes

1 package (18 ounces)
    frozen cut broccoli
2 tablespoons chopped onion
1 tablespoon water
1 tablespoon butter or
    margarine
1 cup dairy sour cream
½ teaspoon celery salt
¼ teaspoon celery seed
⅛ teaspoon white pepper

In 2-quart microproof casserole, combine broccoli, onion, water, and butter. Cook on HI (max. power) 18 to 20 minutes, or until vegetables are tender, stirring once during cooking time. Drain, if necessary. Combine remaining ingredients; stir into broccoli. Cover and let stand 3 minutes before serving.

Creamed Cabbage _____ 6 servings

Total Cooking Time: 8 to 9 minutes

1 teaspoon cornstarch
½ cup milk
6 cups shredded cabbage
1 package (3 ounces) cream
    cheese, cut up
1 tablespoon parsley flakes
1 tablespoon minced onion
1 teaspoon salt
⅛ teaspoon white pepper

Dissolve cornstarch in milk. Combine all ingredients in 2-quart microproof casserole. Cover. Cook on HI (max. power) 8 to 9 minutes, or until cabbage is tender, stirring once during cooking time. Stir and let stand 2 minutes before serving.

White Sauce _____ 1 cup

Total Cooking Time: 8 to 9 minutes

1 cup milk
2 tablespoons butter or
    margarine
2 tablespoons all-purpose
    flour
  Dash white pepper
  Dash grated or ground nutmeg

Pour milk into 2-cup glass measure. Cook on HI (max. power) 2 minutes; set aside. Place butter in 4-cup glass measure. Cook on HI (max. power) 1 minute, or until melted. Stir in flour. Cook on HI (max. power) 1 minute. Briskly stir in warm milk, pepper, and nutmeg. Cook on HI (max. power) 4 to 5 minutes, or until mixture boils, stirring twice during cooking time. Let stand 5 minutes before serving.

For Cheese Sauce, stir ½ to 1 cup shredded cheese into hot sauce until melted.

Potatoes Au Gratin _____ 4 to 5 servings

Total Cooking Time: 20 to 22 minutes

1 package (16 ounces) frozen
   Southern-style hash
   brown potatoes
1 can (10¾ ounces)
   condensed cream of
   potato soup
½ cup dairy sour cream
¾ cup shredded Cheddar
   cheese, divided

In 1¾-quart shallow microproof casserole, combine potatoes, soup, sour cream, and ½ cup cheese; blend well. Cook on HI (max. power) 20 to 22 minutes, or until potatoes are tender, stirring once during cooking time. Sprinkle with remaining ¼ cup cheese. Cover and let stand 3 minutes, or until cheese is melted.

Sliced Oven Fries _____ 4 servings

Total Cooking Time: 15 to 19 minutes

4 medium potatoes, peeled
   and sliced
1 medium onion, sliced
1 teaspoon salt
   Dash freshly ground
   pepper
3 tablespoons butter or
   margarine
   Paprika

Combine potatoes, onion, salt, and pepper in shallow 1-quart microproof casserole. Dot with butter. Cover. Cook on HI (max. power) 15 to 19 minutes, or until potatoes are tender, stirring every 5 minutes. Sprinkle with paprika before serving.

Parslied Potatoes _____ 4 to 6 servings

Total Cooking Time: 16 to 18 minutes

4 medium potatoes
¼ cup water
3 tablespoons butter or
   margarine
3 to 4 tablespoons minced
   fresh parsley
   Salt
   Freshly ground pepper

Peel potatoes and quarter. Combine potatoes and water in 2-quart microproof casserole; cover. Cook on HI (max. power) 16 to 18 minutes, or until tender, stirring once during cooking time; drain. Add butter, parsley, salt, and pepper. Stir until butter is melted. Serve immediately.

You may choose to use 16 whole new potatoes instead of quartering the larger variety.

Hash Brown Potato Bake _____ 6 servings

Total Cooking Time: 22 to 26 minutes

1 package (16 ounces)
    frozen Southern-style
    hash browns
1 can (10¾ ounces) cream
    of potato soup
½ cup dairy sour cream
2 green onions, sliced
½ teaspoon salt
¼ teaspoon freshly ground
    pepper
1 tablespoon minced parsley
    Paprika

In 1½-quart microproof casserole, place frozen potatoes. Cover. Cook on HI (max. power) 8 to 10 minutes. Stir in soup, sour cream, onions, salt, pepper, and parsley. Cover. Cook on HI (max. power) 14 to 16 minutes, stirring once during cooking time. Sprinkle with paprika. Let stand, covered, 5 minutes before serving.

Onion Pie in Rice Crust _____ 6 servings

Total Cooking Time: 21 to 23 minutes

1 Rice Pie Crust (page 158)
1 cup shredded Cheddar
    cheese
1 cup shredded Swiss cheese
¼ cup thinly sliced green
    onion
1 tablespoon butter or
    margarine
1 can (6 ounces) evaporated
    milk
3 eggs
1 teaspoon prepared mustard
½ teaspoon salt
1 can (3 ounces) French-
    fried onions

Sprinkle cheeses in prepared pie crust. In 2-cup glass measure, combine onion and butter. Cook on HI (max. power) 3 minutes, or until onion is transparent, stirring after 1 minute. Add milk. Cook on HI (max. power) 3 minutes, or until milk is heated through.

In small bowl, combine eggs, mustard, and salt; mix lightly. Gradually pour hot milk mixture into egg mixture while beating. Pour carefully over cheese in pie crust. Crumble French-fried onions over top. Cook on HI (max. power) 15 to 17 minutes, or until center is nearly set, rotating dish if pie is cooking unevenly. Cover with aluminum foil; let stand on breadboard or heatproof counter top 10 minutes before serving.

German Potato Salad _____ 5 to 6 servings

Total Cooking Time: 31½ to 37 minutes

4 large potatoes
4 slices bacon
1 medium onion, chopped
1 tablespoon all-purpose
   flour
½ cup water
¼ cup vinegar
¼ cup sugar
1 teaspoon salt
¾ teaspoon paprika
½ teaspoon celery seed
⅛ teaspoon freshly ground
   pepper

Cook potatoes according to Guide on page 66; set aside. Place bacon in 2-quart microproof casserole. Cover with paper toweling. Cook on HI (max. power) 6 to 8 minutes, or until crisp. Remove bacon from casserole; set aside. Reserve 4 tablespoons drippings. Add onion to drippings. Cook on HI (max. power) 2 minutes. Add flour; stir. Cook on HI (max. power) 1 minute, or until onion is transparent. Stir in remaining ingredients. Cook on HI (max. power) 4½ to 5 minutes, or until mixture thickens. Peel and slice potatoes. Add to hot mixture. Stir to coat potatoes with sauce. Crumble bacon over top. Serve warm.

If salad cools, reheat by cooking on HI (max. power) 2 to 3 minutes.

Lemon-Glazed Carrots _____ 4 to 5 servings

Total Cooking Time: 16 to 19 minutes

3 cups (about 10 medium)
   thinly sliced carrots
¼ cup water
¼ cup chopped green pepper
3 tablespoons butter or
   margarine
1 tablespoon lemon juice
½ teaspoon cornstarch
½ teaspoon sugar (optional)
¼ teaspoon grated lemon rind
¼ teaspoon salt
   Dash white pepper

In 1-quart microproof casserole, combine carrots and water. Cover. Cook on HI (max. power) 5 minutes. Stir in green pepper. Cover. Cook on HI (max. power) 10 to 13 minutes, or until carrots are tender, stirring once during cooking time. Drain. In small bowl, combine remaining ingredients; add to carrots. Stir until butter is melted. Cook on HI (max. power) 1 minute, or until sauce is heated through.

German Potato Salad, Lemon-Glazed Carrots→

Denver Scramble _____ 4 to 6 servings

Total Cooking Time: 6 to 7 minutes

4 eggs
¼ cup mayonnaise
¼ cup milk
½ cup minced cooked ham
1 tablespoon instant minced onion
1 tablespoon chopped pimiento
1 tablespoon chopped green pepper
⅛ teaspoon salt
1 small tomato, seeded and chopped
4 to 6 slices toast

Combine eggs, mayonnaise, and milk in 1- to 1½-quart microproof casserole; blend well. Stir in ham, onion, pimiento, green pepper, and salt. Cover. Cook on HI (max. power) 5 to 6 minutes, or until just set, stirring every two mintues during cooking time. Stir in tomato. Cook, covered, on HI (max. power) 1 minute. Let stand 2 minutes.

This recipe can be doubled and cooked in 2-quart microproof casserole. Double cooking time.

Eggs Florentine _____ 4 servings

Total Cooking Time: 31 to 37 minutes

½ package (12 ounces) frozen hash brown potatoes
1 package (10 ounces) frozen chopped spinach
1 tablespoon minced onion
½ teaspoon lemon pepper
½ cup Cheese Sauce (variation, White Sauce, page 73)
4 eggs
1 tablespoon butter or margarine
¼ cup dry bread crumbs

Thaw potatoes and spinach on 50 (defrost) 12 to 15 minutes, or until thawed. Drain spinach well. In 1½-quart oval or round shallow microproof dish, combine potato, spinach, onion, and pepper; set aside. Prepare Cheese Sauce and pour over spinach. Make 4 indentations in spinach mixture; break 1 egg into each. Pierce each yolk. Set aside. Place butter in small microproof dish. Cook on HI (max. power) 1 minute. Stir in bread crumbs. Sprinkle over eggs. Cover with waxed paper. Cook on HI (max. power) 9 to 11 minutes, or until eggs are almost set. Let stand 3 minutes before serving.

Low-Cal Eggs Oriental _____ 2 to 3 servings

Total Cooking Time: 9½ to 10 minutes

1 tablespoon butter or
  margarine
½ cup sliced mushrooms
1 cup chopped green onions
4 eggs
4 tablespoons water
1 can (8 ounces) sliced
  water chestnuts
1 cup alfalfa sprouts
½ teaspoon salt
¼ teaspoon freshly ground
  pepper

Place butter in 8-inch microproof pie plate. Cook on HI (max. power) 1 minute, or until melted. Add mushrooms and onions. Cover with waxed paper. Cook on HI (max. power) 3 minutes. In small bowl, mix remaining ingredients. Add to onions and mushrooms; stir lightly to mix. Cover. Cook on HI (max. power) 5½ to 6 minutes, or until eggs are set, stirring every 2 minutes during cooking time. Let stand 1 to 2 minutes. Sprinkle with additional sprouts. Serve with soy sauce, if desired.

Classic Omelet _____ 2 servings

Total Cooking Time: 7 to 7½ minutes

1 tablespoon butter or
  margarine
4 eggs
4 tablespoons water
½ teaspoon salt
⅛ teaspoon freshly ground
  pepper

Place butter in 9-inch microproof pie plate. Cook on HI (max. power) 1 minute, or until melted. Beat remaining ingredients in bowl; pour into pie plate. Cover with waxed paper. Cook on HI (max. power) 6 to 6½ minutes, stirring once during cooking time. Let stand, covered, 1 to 2 minutes. Fold in half to serve.

Spanish Omelet _____ 4 servings

Total Cooking Time: 14½ to 15 minutes

1 tablespoon butter or
    margarine
½ cup chopped onion
⅓ cup chopped green pepper
1 cup tomato sauce or
    tomatoes with bits
½ teaspoon salt
¼ to ½ teaspoon
    hot pepper sauce
2 Classic Omelets (page 79)

In 4-cup glass measure, combine butter, onion, and green pepper. Cook on HI (max. power) 3½ minutes, or until onion is transparent. Add remaining ingredients, except omelets. Cook on HI (max. power) 4 minutes, or until mixture boils.

Prepare Classic Omelets. Before folding in half, spoon one-fourth of the tomato mixture on each omelet. Serve topped with remaining mixture.

Jelly Omelet _____ 2 servings

Total Cooking Time: 5¾ to 6¼ minutes

1 tablespoon butter or
    margarine
4 eggs
4 tablespoons water
½ teaspoon salt
⅛ teaspoon freshly ground
    pepper
⅓ cup currant or other
    tart jelly

Place butter in 9-inch microproof pie plate. Cook on HI (max. power) 45 seconds, or until melted. In small bowl, beat remaining ingredients, except jelly, with fork. Pour into pie plate. Cover with waxed paper. Cook on HI (max. power) 3 minutes, stirring once during cooking time. Cover. Cook on 60 (braise) 2 to 2½ minutes; stir. Let stand, covered, 1 to 2 minutes. Spread jelly over bottom half of omelet; fold top half over jelly. Cut in half. Serve hot.

Fiesta Pie _____ 2 to 3 servings

Total Cooking Time: 6 to 6½ minutes

1 tablespoon butter or
   margarine
4 eggs
4 tablespoons water
2 tablespoons chopped mild
   green chilies
1½ teaspoons onion flakes
½ teaspoon chili powder
½ teaspoon salt
¼ teaspoon freshly ground
   pepper
½ cup shredded sharp
   Cheddar cheese
1 medium tomato, cut in
   wedges

Place butter in 8-inch microproof pie plate. Cook on HI (max. power) 1 minute, or until melted. In small bowl, combine remaining ingredients, except cheese and tomato. Pour into pie plate. Cover with waxed paper. Cook on HI (max. power) 3 minutes. Stir lightly; cook on HI (max. power) 2 to 2½ minutes, or until eggs are almost set in center. Sprinkle with cheese. Let stand, covered, 5 minutes, or until cheese is melted. Serve garnished with tomato wedges.

Cheese Fondue _____ 4 to 6 servings

Total Cooking Time: 7 to 9 minutes

1 pound (4 cups) shredded
   Swiss cheese
2 tablespoons cornstarch
1½ cups dry white wine
1 small clove garlic, minced
   Dash salt
   Freshly ground pepper
   French bread, cut in cubes
   Assorted vegetables

Combine cheese and cornstarch in 2-quart microproof casserole. Stir in wine, garlic, salt, and pepper. Cook on HI (max. power) 7 to 9 minutes, or until cheese is melted and smooth, stirring twice during cooking time. Pour into fondue pot and keep warm. If mixture becomes too thick, add more wine. Serve with bread cubes and assorted vegetables.

ONE-DISH DINNERS

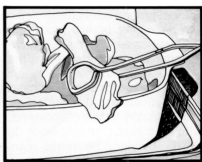

Some casseroles need occasional stirring. Use hot pads when the dish is hot (left). Large items, such as chicken pieces, are rearranged using tongs (above).

By now, we think you should have a pretty good notion about the speed of microwave cooking. But let's not forget those time-saving and tasty casseroles, perhaps the first cooking shortcuts in conventional cooking. No doubt the first "casserole" was developed over an open fire!

It probably won't surprise you either to learn that the microwave oven is specially suited to casserole cooking. Convenience plus speed make those one-dish wonders better than ever.

Because no heat is applied to the casserole dish, food does not stick. And, of course, you can do ingredient preparation, such as sautéing onions or pre-cooking meat, right in the same dish in the microwave oven. No stovetop steps at all!

We've assembled a balanced collection of some traditional casseroles plus a few unique ideas. We hope you will want to try all of them.

Converting Your Recipes

It's so easy to convert your own casserole recipes that you'll probably need to adjust only three items, if at all. They are: a reduction in the amount of liquid because little evaporation occurs in the microwave oven; changing from long-grain rice or dried beans to quick-cooking or precooked, canned types; and, doing some steps first, such as cooking onion to be sure it is tender. For more help, read the casserole information on page 31 and these tips:

☐ Most ground beef casseroles call for extra lean meat. If you are using regular ground beef, partially cook and then drain fat before adding other ingredients.
☐ Many casserole dishes have their own lids. However, often those lids, especially decorative ones, make large casseroles too tall for the oven. When necessary, cover with plastic wrap instead.
☐ With the microwave oven, casseroles can go right from the freezer to the oven for defrosting and cooking. For a 2-quart casserole, cook on 50 (defrost) 15 to 18 minutes. Let stand, covered, for 5 minutes. Stir. Cook on HI (max. power) 12 to 15 minutes, stirring twice during cooking.
☐ The temperature probe can be used to determine precise casserole temperatures. 150°F is the recommended temperature.

Bavarian Wiener Supper _____ 5 to 6 servings
Total Cooking Time: 14 to 17 minutes

1 pound (about 10) frankfurters
1 can (10¾ ounces) condensed cream of mushroom soup
½ cup mayonnaise
1 can (14 ounces) sauerkraut, drained
1 teaspoon caraway seeds
4 cups diced cooked potatoes
½ cup buttered bread crumbs
¼ teaspoon paprika

Cut 3 of the frankfurters in half lengthwise; set aside. Slice remaining frankfurters ¼ inch thick. In small bowl, combine soup and mayonnaise; set aside. In shallow 2-quart microproof casserole, combine sauerkraut, caraway, sliced frankfurters, and half of soup mixture; spread evenly. In separate bowl, mix remaining soup mixture with potatoes; spoon around edges of dish. Sprinkle bread crumbs over potatoes. Sprinkle with paprika. Arrange halved frankfurters decoratively in center. Cook on HI (max. power) 14 to 17 minutes, or until heated through. Let stand 3 minutes before serving.

Ground Beef Gumbo _____ 4 to 5 servings

Total Cooking Time: 15 minutes

1 pound lean ground beef
1/4 cup chopped onion
2 tablespoons chopped green
    pepper
1 can (10¾ ounces) chicken
    gumbo soup
1/4 teaspoon salt
1/8 teaspoon freshly ground
    pepper
2 cups hot cooked rice

Combine beef, onion, and green pepper in 2-quart microproof casserole. Cook on HI (max. power) 10 minutes, or until beef is no longer red, stirring once during cooking. Break up beef with fork; drain. Stir in remaining ingredients, except rice. Cover. Cook on HI (max. power) 5 minutes, stirring once during cooking time. Serve over rice.

Ground Beef Gumbo can also be served as a sandwich filling in hamburger buns.

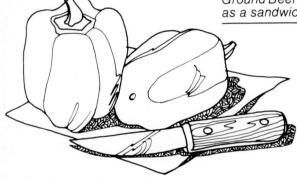

Cowboy Beef Casserole _____ 5 to 6 servings

Total Cooking Time: 17 to 19 minutes

1 pound lean ground beef
1/4 cup chopped onion
1/4 cup chopped green pepper
1 can (16 ounces) tomatoes,
    drained and diced,
    liquid reserved
1 can (12 ounces) whole
    kernel corn, drained
1 can (8 ounces) tomato
    sauce
1/2 cup sliced stuffed olives
1 to 2 teaspoons chili
    powder
1 cup coarsely crushed corn
    chips
1/2 cup shredded Cheddar
    cheese

Place beef in 2-quart microproof casserole; break up with fork. Add onion and green pepper. Cook on HI (max. power) 9 minutes, or until beef is no longer red; drain. Stir to break up beef. Add tomatoes to meat mixture. Stir in 1/4 cup reserved tomato liquid, corn, tomato sauce, olives, and chili powder. Cover. Cook on HI (max. power) 6 to 8 minutes, or until heated through; stir. Sprinkle with corn chips and cheese. Cook on 50 (defrost) 2 minutes, or until cheese is melted. Let stand 3 minutes before serving.

Italian Beef Casserole _____ 6 to 8 servings

Total Cooking Time: 26 to 30 minutes

1 pound lean ground beef
1 can (15½ ounces)
    spaghetti sauce
1¼ cups water
1 can (16 ounces) cut green
    beans, drained
1 package (7 ounces) elbow
    macaroni
2 tablespoons dry onion
    flakes
1 tablespoon sugar
1 tablespoon Italian
    seasoning
½ teaspoon garlic powder
½ teaspoon salt
⅛ teaspoon freshly ground
    pepper
1 cup shredded mozzarella
    cheese

Place ground beef in shallow 3-quart microproof casserole; break up with fork. Cook on HI (max. power) 5 to 7 minutes, or until beef is no longer red. Break up any large pieces; drain. Add remaining ingredients, except cheese; mix well. Cover. Cook on HI (max. power) 9 minutes. Stir; cover. Cook on HI (max. power) 12 to 14 minutes, or until noodles are cooked. Sprinkle with cheese. Cover and let stand 10 minutes before serving.

Beefburger Stroganoff _____ 6 servings

Total Cooking Time: 19 to 21 minutes

1 pound lean ground beef
1 small onion, chopped
1 clove garlic, minced
1 can (10¾ ounces)
    condensed cream of
    chicken soup
1 can (8 ounces) mushroom
    stems and pieces,
    drained
2 tablespoons tomato paste
¼ teaspoon salt
⅛ teaspoon freshly ground
    pepper
1 cup dairy sour cream
2 tablespoons chopped
    fresh parsley
4 cups hot cooked rice
    or noodles

Place ground beef in 2-quart microproof casserole; break up with fork. Stir in onion and garlic. Cook on HI (max. power) 8 to 10 minutes, or until beef is no longer red and onion is transparent; drain. Stir in soup, mushrooms, tomato paste, salt, and pepper. Cover. Cook on HI (max. power) 10 minutes, stirring once. Stir in sour cream. Cook on HI (max. power) 1 minute; stir. Sprinkle with parsley. Serve over rice or noodles.

Garlic Bread (page 159), Italian Beef Casserole→

Chili Beef and Chips ————————— 6 to 8 servings

Total Cooking Time: 24 to 26 minutes

1 pound lean ground beef
½ cup chopped onion
1 clove garlic, minced
1 can (10¾ ounces) condensed cream of mushroom soup
1 can (4 ounces) chopped green chilies
1 package (6¼ ounces) corn or tortilla chips
1 can (10 ounces) mild enchilada sauce
2 cups shredded Cheddar cheese
2 tablespoons chopped black olives

Place ground beef in 2-quart micro-proof casserole; break up with fork. Add onion and garlic. Cook on HI (max. power) 9 minutes, or until beef is no longer red and onion is transparent. Stir to break up meat; drain. Stir in soup and chilies. In 10×8×2-inch oval microproof casserole, place about 2 cups corn chips. Layer half each of the meat mixture, enchilada sauce, and cheese. Repeat. Cook on HI (max. power) 15 to 17 minutes, or until heated through. Sprinkle with remaining corn chips and olives. Let stand 3 minutes before serving.

Stuffed Cabbage Roll Casserole ————————————— 8 servings

Total Cooking Time: 33½ to 38½ minutes

8 large cabbage leaves (use outer leaves)
½ cup water
1 pound lean ground beef
3 tablespoons chopped onion
1 cup quick-cooking rice
1 egg, slightly beaten
1 teaspoon salt
⅛ teaspoon freshly ground pepper
1½ cups tomato juice
1 can (10½ ounces) pizza sauce
1 teaspoon sugar
½ teaspoon oregano

Place cabbage leaves and water in 2-quart microproof casserole. Cover. Cook on HI (max. power) 7½ to 9½ minutes, or until leaves are pliable. Place ground beef in 4-cup glass measure; break up with fork. Stir in onion. Cook on HI (max. power) 5 minutes, or until beef is partially cooked and onion is transparent; drain and cool. Stir in rice, egg, salt, and pepper. Drain cabbage. Divide beef mixture (about ⅓ cup) among cabbage leaves, spooning onto center of each. Roll up; secure with toothpick, if necessary. Place cabbage rolls in 3-quart casserole, seam-side down.

In small bowl, blend tomato juice, pizza sauce, sugar, and oregano. Pour over cabbage rolls; cover. Cook on HI (max. power) 21 to 24 minutes, or until tender, rearranging cabbage rolls and basting with sauce after 10 minutes.

Supper Pie _____ 6 servings

Total Cooking Time: 21 to 23 minutes

1 package (8 ounces)
   spaghetti, cooked
1 egg, slightly beaten
⅓ cup grated Parmesan
   cheese
1 tablespoon butter or
   margarine
1 tablespoon parsley flakes
¾ pound lean ground beef
1 onion, finely chopped
1 clove garlic, minced
1 can (8 ounces) whole
   tomatoes, drained
   and cut in pieces,
   liquid reserved
1 can (6 ounces) tomato
   paste
½ teaspoon oregano
½ teaspoon salt
¼ teaspoon freshly ground
   pepper
1 cup ricotta cheese
½ cup shredded Monterey
   Jack or mozzarella
   cheese

In large bowl, combine spaghetti, egg, Parmesan cheese, butter, and parsley; stir until butter is melted. Turn into 10-inch microproof pie plate; press mixture evenly onto bottom and sides. Cook on HI (max. power) 2 minutes, rotating after 1 minute; set aside.

Combine ground beef, onion, and garlic in 2-quart microproof bowl; break up beef with fork. Cook on HI (max. power) 8 to 9 minutes, or until beef is no longer red; drain. Add tomatoes, tomato paste, oregano, salt, and pepper. Cook on HI (max. power) 4 minutes.

Spread ricotta cheese over spaghetti; pour meat mixture over ricotta cheese. Cover with waxed paper. Cook on HI (max. power) 7 to 8 minutes, or until heated through. Sprinkle with shredded cheese. Cover and let stand 3 minutes until cheese is melted. Serve hot.

Macaroni and Cheese _____ 4 to 6 servings

Total Cooking Time: 11½ to 13½ minutes

2 cups elbow macaroni
2 tablespoons butter or
   margarine
2 tablespoons flour
2 cups milk
1 teaspoon salt
1 tablespoon instant minced
   onion
2 cups shredded Cheddar
   cheese

Cook macaroni according to package directions; drain. Place in 2-quart microproof casserole; set aside. Place butter in 2-quart microproof casserole. Cook on HI (max. power) 1 minute, or until melted. Stir in flour until blended.

Pour milk into 2-cup glass measure. Cook on HI (max. power) 2½ minutes. Stir into flour-butter mixture. Cook on HI (max. power) 8 to 10 minutes, or until thickened, stirring frequently. Add salt and onion. Add cheese; stir until melted. Pour over macaroni; blend well. Serve immediately.

Ham, Asparagus, and Noodle Casserole _____ 6 servings

Total Cooking Time: 9½ to 12 minutes

2 cups cooked noodles
1 tablespoon parsley flakes
1 cup milk
2 tablespoons butter or margarine
2 tablespoons all-purpose flour
½ teaspoon salt
¼ teaspoon white pepper
1 package (3 ounces) cream cheese, cut up
3 teaspoons prepared mustard
6 slices boiled ham
1 can (14½ ounces) asparagus spears or 18 fresh asparagus spears, cooked and drained
Paprika

Combine noodles with parsley; mix lightly; set aside.

Pour milk into 2-cup glass measure. Cook on HI (max. power) 2 minutes, or until heated through; set aside. Place butter in another 2-cup glass measure. Cook on HI (max. power) 1 minute. Stir in flour; blend well. Cook on HI (max. power) 1 minute. Briskly stir in warm milk, salt, and pepper. Cook on HI (max. power) 2½ to 3 minutes, or until boiling and thickened, stirring once during cooking. Stir in cream cheese until melted.

Pour half of sauce over noodles; stir to coat. Spread noodle mixture in shallow 1½-quart round or oval micro-proof dish.

Spread ½ teaspoon mustard on each ham slice. Roll up 3 asparagus spears in each ham slice. Place ham rolls, seam-side down, over noodles. Pour remaining sauce over ham. Sprinkle with paprika. Cook on HI (max. power) 5 to 7 minutes, or until heated through. Let stand 2 minutes before serving.

Chicken and Rice Casserole _____ 4 to 6 servings

Total Cooking Time: 18 to 20 minutes

2 cups boned chicken, cut in 1-inch cubes
1 can (10¾ ounces) condensed cream of chicken soup
1 cup milk
1 cup sliced mushrooms
⅔ cup quick-cooking rice
1 envelope dry onion soup mix
¼ teaspoon poultry seasoning
½ cup shredded Cheddar cheese

Combine all ingredients, except cheese, in 1½-quart microproof casserole. Cover with plastic wrap. Cook on HI (max. power) 18 to 20 minutes, stirring twice during cooking time. Sprinkle with cheese. Cover and let stand 10 minutes before serving.

←*Ham, Asparagus, and Noodle Casserole*

Cantonese Beef and Vegetables

4 to 5 servings

Total Cooking Time: 13½ to 16½ minutes

¼ cup dry sherry
¼ cup soy sauce
¼ cup water
1 tablespoon sugar
1 clove garlic, minced
1 pound boneless beef steak, such as sirloin, thinly sliced
6 green onions
1 small head cauliflower
1 package (7 ounces) frozen pea pods
1 can (5 ounces) sliced water chestnuts, drained

In 2-quart microproof dish, combine sherry, soy sauce, water, sugar, and garlic. Add beef; stir. Cover with plastic wrap. Let stand, at room temperature, 4 hours, stirring occasionally.

Cut onions, white and green part, in 2-inch pieces; split lengthwise; set aside. Separate cauliflower into florets; slice each ¼-inch thick; set aside. Stir onions and cauliflower into beef mixture. Cover. Cook on HI (max. power) 11 to 13 minutes, stirring once during cooking time. Stir in frozen pea pods and water chestnuts. Cover. Cook on HI (max. power) 2½ to 3½ minutes, or until pea pods and cauliflower are crisp-tender. Serve over hot cooked rice.

Hearty Beef Vegetable Stew

6 to 8 servings

Total Cooking Time: 42 to 47 minutes

2¼ cups water, divided
2 beef bouillon cubes
1 pound round steak, cut in ½-inch cubes
3 tablespoons cornstarch
2 large potatoes, peeled and cubed
¾ cup thinly sliced carrots
½ cup thinly sliced celery
1 medium onion, diced
½ teaspoon salt
¼ teaspoon freshly ground pepper
¼ teaspoon thyme
1 bay leaf, crushed

Combine 2 cups of the water, bouillon cubes, and beef in 2-quart microproof bowl. Cook on HI (max. power) 17 minutes, or until steak is tender. In 1-cup microproof measure, mix remaining ¼ cup water and cornstarch. Add cornstarch and remaining ingredients to beef; stir. Cover with waxed paper. Cook on HI (max. power) 25 to 30 minutes, or until vegetables are tender, stirring twice during cooking time. Cover and let stand 10 minutes before serving.

Ham and Potato Scallop _____ 4 servings

Total Cooking Time: 24 to 26 minutes

1 cup milk
2 tablespoons butter or
   margarine
2 tablespoons all-purpose
   flour
1 teaspoon prepared mustard
½ teaspoon salt
¼ teaspoon white pepper
3 medium potatoes, peeled
   and thinly sliced
   (about 1½ cups)
1½ cups cooked diced ham
1 teaspoon minced onion
¼ cup shredded Cheddar
   cheese

Pour milk into 2-cup glass measure. Cook on HI (max. power) 2 minutes; set aside. Place butter in 2-cup glass measure. Cook on HI (max. power) 1 minute. Stir in flour. Cook on HI (max. power) 1 minute. Briskly stir hot milk, prepared mustard, salt, and pepper into butter. Set aside. Place potatoes in 1½-quart microproof casserole. Add ham and onion. Pour white sauce over ham and potatoes mixture; stir to combine. Cover with waxed paper. Cook on HI (max. power) 20 to 22 minutes, stirring twice during cooking time. Sprinkle with cheese. Cover and let stand 10 minutes, or until cheese is melted.

Chicken and Spinach Casserole _____ 4 servings

Total Cooking Time: 25 to 28 minutes

4 tablespoons butter or
   margarine, divided
½ cup chopped onion
2 packages (10 ounces each)
   frozen chopped
   spinach, thawed and
   thoroughly drained
2 cups diced cooked
   chicken
1 can (10¾ ounces)
   condensed cream of
   chicken soup
1 cup shredded Swiss cheese
3 tablespoons chicken broth
⅔ cup bread crumbs
   Paprika

In 1-cup glass measure, combine 1 tablespoon butter with onion. Cook on HI (max. power) 3 to 4 minutes, or until onion is tender. Stir onion into spinach. Spread mixture in 9-inch pie plate. Spoon chicken evenly over spinach. Set aside. Combine soup, cheese, and broth in 4-cup glass measure. Cook on HI (max. power) 6 minutes; stir to melt cheese. Pour evenly over chicken. Combine bread crumbs and remaining 3 tablespoons butter in 2-cup glass measure. Cook on HI (max. power) 2 minutes; stir to blend. Sprinkle bread crumbs on top. Sprinkle with paprika. Cook on HI (max. power) 14 to 16 minutes, rotating once during cooking time.

Stir-Fry Shrimp and Vegetables _____ 4 servings

Total Cooking Time: 10 to 11 minutes

1 tablespoon cornstarch
¾ cup water
2 tablespoons soy sauce
¼ teaspoon bead molasses
2 cups broccoli florets
1 can (4¼ ounces) large shrimp, drained
1 small onion, diced
2 cups hot cooked rice

Mix together cornstarch, water, soy sauce, and molasses; set aside. Combine broccoli, shrimp, and onions in 1-quart microproof casserole; add sauce mixture. Cook on HI (max. power) 6 minutes, stirring halfway through cooking time. Stir; cover with waxed paper. Cook on HI (max. power) 4 to 5 minutes, or until broccoli is crisp-tender. Cover and let stand 5 minutes before serving. Serve over rice.

Tuna-Cashew Casserole _____ 5 to 6 servings

Total Cooking Time: 12 to 16 minutes

1 can (10¾ ounces) condensed cream of mushroom soup
¾ cup milk
3 cups cooked noodles
1 can (6½ ounces) tuna, drained and flaked
½ cup diced celery
½ cup broken salted cashew nuts
1 tablespoon instant minced onion
½ teaspoon salt
⅛ teaspoon freshly ground pepper
¼ cup crushed soda crackers

Blend soup and milk in 2-quart microproof casserole. Add remaining ingredients, except crackers; blend well. Cook on HI (max. power) 8 to 10 minutes; stir. Top with cracker crumbs. Cook on HI (max. power) 4 to 6 minutes, or until hot in center.

BUDGET-WISE MEAT

Arrangement is important when cooking meat (left). A microwave food thermometer is helpful in determining preferred doneness for meat loaf (above).

Cooking meat in the microwave oven offers tremendous advantages over the conventional range. In today's economy, we need all the help we can get and the microwave stretches your dollar by reducing meat shrinkage.

If you have varying doneness preferences at your table, the microwave solves the problem nicely. After a roast is carved, a few seconds in the microwave oven will bring slices of rare meat to medium or well done.

Some people believe that meat does not brown in microwave ovens. They are mistaken. Any meat that cooks more than 10 minutes will brown in your microwave oven. It is true that individual steaks, chops, and thin cuts of meat that cook quickly will brown best with a microproof browning dish (see the photograph on page 45).

Try our attractive Polynesian Pork Kabobs (page 108), Super Meat Loaf Ring (page 104), or Pot Roast and Vegetables (page 106).

Converting Your Recipes

Charts on the following pages outline microwave thawing and cooking times for the standard cuts of meat. For converting meat loaf, meat in sauces, and recipes that call for less tender cuts of meat, you're sure to find a similar recipe here to guide your own creations. Adapt your conventional recipes by matching ingredients' and methods as closely as possible. Experiment as much as you like. Here are some helpful hints:

If you don't have a microproof ring mold, you can make one easily. Insert a small straight-sided glass, open-end up, in the center of a glass or ceramic round baking dish.

☐ Recipe times here presume meat is at refrigerator temperature. If your meal requires lengthy preparation, during which the meat may reach room temperature, reduce cooking times.

☐ Baste, marinate, or season meat just as you would for conventional cooking. However, avoid salting the surface before or during cooking, since salt tends to draw liquids from food.

☐ You can use a microwave roasting rack to elevate meat from its drippings during cooking.

☐ Check dishes that use relatively long cooking times to be sure liquid has not evaporated. Add liquid as necessary.

☐ You can enhance the color and flavor of steaks, meat loaf, and roasts by using one of the following: powdered brown gravy mix; a liquid browning agent; Worcestershire sauce, soy sauce, or steak sauce; paprika; cooked bacon; tomato sauce; or dehydrated onion soup mix.

The Defrosting Guide

1. Remove meat from its original closed package to provide more even thawing. Remove all metal rings, wire twist ties, and all foil wrapping.

2. Place meat in microproof dish.

3. Defrost in the microwave oven only as long as necessary, since standing time will complete the thawing process.

4. Slightly increase the time for weights larger than on the chart. Do not double.

DEFROSTING GUIDE — MEAT

Meat	Amount	Control	Time (minutes per pound)	Standing Time (minutes)	Special Notes
Beef					
Ground beef	1 lb.	50 (defrost)	8 - 10	5	Turn over once Remove thawed portions with fork Return remainder Freeze in doughnut shape
	2 lbs.	50 (defrost)	7 - 9	5	
	½-lb. patty	50 (defrost)	2 per patty	5	Depress center when freezing Defrost on plate.
Pot roast, chuck	under 4 lbs.	50 (defrost)	3 - 5	10	Turn over once.
Rib roast rolled	3 to 4 lbs.	50 (defrost)	7 - 9	30 - 45	Turn over once.
Rib roast, bone in		HI (max. power)	5 - 7	45 - 90	Turn over twice.
Rump roast	3 to 4 lbs.	50 (defrost)	3 - 5	30	Turn over once.
Round steak		50 (defrost)	7 - 9	5 - 10	Turn over once.
Flank steak		50 (defrost)	7 - 9	5 - 10	Turn over once.
Sirloin steak	½" thick	50 (defrost)	7 - 9	5 - 10	Turn over once.
Tenderloin, whole	2 to 3 lbs.	50 (defrost)	7 - 9	10	Turn over once.
steak	12 oz.	50 (defrost)	5 - 7	8 - 10	Turn over once.
Stew beef	2 lbs.	50 (defrost)	6 - 8	8 - 10	Turn over once. Separate.
Lamb					
Cubed for stew		50 (defrost)	9 - 11	5	Turn over once. Separate.
Ground lamb	under 4 lbs.	50 (defrost)	6 - 8	30 - 45	Turn over once.
Chops	1" thick	50 (defrost)	7 - 9	15	Turn over twice.
Leg	5 - 8 lbs.	50 (defrost)	4 - 5	15 - 20	Turn over twice.
Pork					
Chops	½"	50 (defrost)	5 - 7	5 - 10	Separate chops halfway
	1"	50 (defrost)	6 - 8½	10	through defrosting time.
Spareribs, country-style ribs		50 (defrost)	7 - 9	10	Turn over once.
Roast	under 4 lbs.	50 (defrost)	7 - 9	30 - 45	Turn over twice.
Bacon	1 lb.	50 (defrost)	3 - 5	3 - 5	Defrost until strips separate.
Sausage, bulk	1 lb.	50 (defrost)	3 - 4	3 - 5	Turn over once. Remove thawed portions with fork. Return remainder.
Sausage links	1 lb.	50 (defrost)	3 - 5	4 - 6	Turn over once. Defrost until pieces can be separated.
Hot dogs		50 (defrost)	4 - 6	5	
Veal					
Roast	3 to 4 lbs.	50 (defrost)	5 - 7	30	Turn over once.
Chops	½" thick	50 (defrost)	4 - 6	20	Turn over once Separate chops and continue defrosting.
Variety Meat					
Liver		50 (defrost)	4 - 6	10	Turn over once.
Tongue		50 (defrost)	7 - 9	10	Turn over once.

Using the Cooking Guide

1. Meat should be completely thawed before cooking.
2. Place meat, fat-side down, on microwave roasting rack set in glass baking dish. An inverted microproof saucer may be used if you do not have a roasting rack.
3. Meat may be covered lightly with waxed paper to stop splatters.
4. Use a microwave meat thermometer for the most accurate cooking of larger meat cuts.
5. Unless otherwise noted, times given for steaks and patties will give medium doneness.
6. During standing time, the internal temperature of roasts will rise approximately 15°F. Hence, standing time is considered an essential part of the time required to complete cooking.
7. Cutlets and chops that are breaded are cooked in the same time as shown on chart.
8. Check the size of your oven before purchasing meat.

COOKING GUIDE — MEAT
Cook on HI (max. power).

Meat	First Cook Time	Second Cook Time	Standing Time (minutes)	Special Notes
Beef				
Ground beef bulk	3 minutes per pound	Stir. 3 minutes per pound	5	Crumble in dish, cook covered.
Ground beef patty, 4 oz. 1/2" thick	1 1/2 - 2 minutes	Turn over. 1 - 2 minutes		Shallow baking dish
2	2 1/2 - 3 minutes	Turn over. 2 - 3 minutes		Shallow baking dish.
4	4 1/2 minutes	Turn over. 4 - 5 minutes		Shallow baking dish.
Meat loaf 2 lbs.	20-24 minutes		5 - 10	Glass loaf dish or glass ring mold.
Beef rib roast, boneless	Rare: 5 1/2 - 6 minutes per pound Medium: 6 1/2 - 8 minutes per pound Well: 8 - 9 1/2 minutes per pound	Turn over. 4 - 5 minutes per pound 6 minutes per pound 7 - 8 minutes per pound	10 10 10	Glass baking dish with microproof roasting rack.
Rib roast, bone in	Rare: 4 - 5 1/2 minutes per pound Medium: 5 1/2 - 6 1/2 minutes per pound Well: 6 1/2 - 8 minutes per pound	Turn over. 4 - 5 minutes per pound 4 - 6 minutes per pound 6 - 7 minutes per pound	10	Glass baking dish with microproof roasting rack.

COOKING GUIDE — MEAT is continued on page 99→

Meat	First Cook Time	Second Cook Time	Standing Time (minutes)	Special Notes
Beef round, rump, or chuck, boneless	6 minutes per pound	Turn over. 75 (simmer) 20 minutes per pound	10-15	2-quart casserole with tight cover. Water to cover.
Beef brisket, boneless, fresh or corned 2½-3½ lbs.	6 minutes per pound	Turn over. 75 (simmer) 20 minutes per pound	10-15	4-quart casserole Dutch oven with tight cover. Water to cover.
Top round steak	6 minutes per pound	Turn over. 75 (simmer) 5 minutes per pound	10-15	Casserole with tight cover. Requires liquid.
Sirloin steak ¾-1″ thick	6 minutes per pound	Drain dish and turn over. 2 minutes per pound	10-15	Shallow cooking dish or browning dish preheated on HI (max. power) 11 minutes.
Minute steak or cube steak 4, 6 oz. steaks	1-2 minutes	Drain dish and turn over. 1½-2½ minutes		Browning dish preheated on HI (max. power) 11 minutes.
Tenderloin	Rare: 3 minutes Med: 4 minutes Well: 6 minutes	Drain, turn steak. 1-1½ minutes 1½-2 minutes 2½-4 minutes	10-15	Browning dish preheated on HI (max. power) 11 minutes.
Rib eye or strip steak 1½-2 lbs.	Rare: 4 minutes Med: 5 minutes Well: 8 minutes	Drain, turn steak. 1-1½ minutes 1½-2½ minutes 2½-4 minutes	10-15	Browning dish preheated on HI (max. power) 11 minutes.
Lamb Ground lamb patties 1-2 lbs.	5 minutes	Turn over. 5½-6½ minutes		Browning dish preheated on HI (max. power) 10 minutes.
Lamb chops 1-1½ lbs. 1″ thick	10 minutes	Turn over 9-10 minutes		Browning dish preheated on HI (max. power) 10 minutes.
Lamb leg or shoulder roast, bone in	Medium: 4-5 minutes per pound Well: 5-6 minutes per pound	Cover end of leg bone with foil. Turn over. Medium: 4-5 minutes per pound Well: 5-6 minutes per pound	5 10	6 × 9-inch dish with microproof roasting rack.
Lamb roast, boneless	6-7 minutes per pound	Turn over. 6-7 minutes per pound	10	6 × 9-inch dish with microproof roasting rack.
Veal Shoulder or rump roast, boneless 2-4 lbs.	9 minutes per pound	Turn over. 10-12 minutes per pound	10	6 × 9-inch dish with microproof roasting rack.
Veal cutlets or loin chops ½″ thick	2 minutes per pound	Turn over 2-5 minutes per pound		Browning dish preheated on HI (max. power) 10-12 minutes.

COOKING GUIDE — MEAT is continued on page 100→

Meat	First Cook Time	Second Cook Time	Standing Time (minutes)	Special Notes
Pork Pork chops 1/2" thick	6 minutes per pound	Turn over. 5-6 minutes per pound	5	Browning dish preheated on HI (max. power) 10 minutes.
Spareribs	7-8 minutes per pound	Turn over. 7-8 minutes per pound	10	6 × 9-inch dish with microproof roasting rack.
Pork loin roast, boneless 3-4 lbs.	7 minutes per pound	Turn over. 6-7 minutes per pound	10	6 × 9-i9nch dish with microproof roasting rack.
Pork loin, center cut 4 lbs.	6-8 minutes per pound	Turn over. 4-6 minutes per pound	10	6 × 9-inch dish with microproof roasting rack.
Center cut ham slice 1-1½ lbs.	6 minutes per pound	Turn over. 6-7 minutes per pound	10	6 × 9-inch baking dish.
Canned ham 3 lbs.	6-7 minutes per pound	6-7 minutes per pound	10	6 × 9-inch dish with microproof roasting rack.
4 lbs.	4-6 minutes per pound	Turn over. 4-6 minutes per pound	10	6 × 9-inch dish with microproof roasting rack.
Sausage patties 12 oz	2 minutes	Turn over. 1½-2 minutes per pound		Browning dish preheated on HI (max. Power) 10 minutes.
Sausage 16 oz.	4 minutes	Stir. 2½-3½ minutes		Crumble into 1½-quart dish, covered.
Bratwurst, precooked	Pierce casing. 6 minutes per pound	Rearrange. 5-6 minutes per pound		Casserole.
Hot dogs 1 2 4	30-45 seconds 50-60 seconds 1-1½ minutes			Shallow dish. Shallow dish. Shallow dish.
Bacon 2 slices	3 minutes			Dish: slices between paper towels.
4 slices	5-6 minutes			Dish; slices between paper towels.
6 slices	7 minutes 8-10 minutes			Roasting rack, slices covered with paper towels.

Special Tips about Bacon

☐ Cook bacon on paper-lined plate, and cover with paper towels to prevent splatters and absorb drippings.

☐ To reserve drippings, cook bacon on a meat rack in a baking dish or on a microwave bacon rack. Bacon can also be cooked, in slices or cut up, in a casserole and removed if necessary with a slotted spoon.

☐ For bacon that is soft rather than crisp, cook at the minimum timing.

☐ Bacon varies in quality. The thickness and amount of sugar and salt used in curing will affect browning and timing. Cook thicker slices a bit longer than the chart indicates. You will also find that sweeter bacon cooks more quickly.

☐ Sugar in bacon causes brown spots to appear on the paper towels. If the bacon tends to stick a bit to the towel, it is due to an extra high amount of sugar.

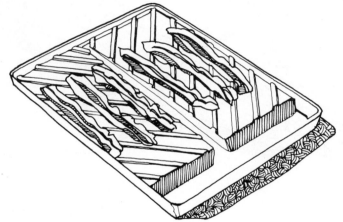

COOKING/DEFROSTING GUIDE — CONVENIENCE BEEF

Food	Amount	Power Control Setting	Time (minutes)	Special Notes
Barbecued beef, Chili, stew, hash, meatballs, etc.	16 oz. or less (cans)	HI (max. power)	4-6	Remove from cans to microproof plate or casserole, cover, Stir halfway through cooking time.
Stuffed peppers, cabbage rolls, chow mein, etc.	16 - 32 oz. (cans)	HI (max. power)	5-9	
Barbecued beef, chili, stew, corned beef hash, meatballs, patties in sauce, gravy	8 - 16 oz. package (frozen)	HI (max. power)	7-15	Remove from foil container to microproof casserole, cover. Slit plastic pouches.
Dry casserole mixes, cooked hamburger added	6½ - 8 oz. package	HI (max. power)	25-30	Remove mix from package to 2-quart microproof casserole. Cover. Stir once.

Porcupine Meatballs _____ 5 to 6 servings

Total Cooking Time: 16 to 17 minutes

- 1 pound lean ground beef
- ½ cup quick-cooking rice
- ¼ cup instant minced onion
- 2 tablespoons minced green pepper
- 1 egg, slightly beaten
- 1 teaspoon salt
- ⅛ teaspoon freshly ground pepper
- 1 can (10¾ ounces) condensed cream of tomato soup
- 1 cup water

In small mixing bowl, combine beef, rice, onion, green pepper, egg, salt, and pepper; blend thoroughly. Form into 24 1-inch balls. Arrange in 2-quart microproof casserole. Blend soup and water; pour over meatballs. Cover. Cook on HI (max. power) 16 to 17 minutes, or until beef is no longer red and rice is tender, rearranging meatballs once during cooking time. Let stand 3 minutes. Remove meatballs with slotted spoon. Pour a small amount of sauce over meatballs. Pass remaining sauce, if desired.

Spicy Stuffed Peppers ——————— 5 servings

Total Cooking Time: 25 to 27 minutes

5 green peppers, tops
   removed and seeded
¾ pound lean ground beef
1 cup quick-cooking rice
¼ cup finely chopped onion
½ teaspoon salt
¼ teaspoon freshly ground
   pepper
¼ teaspoon garlic powder
1 can (8 ounces) tomato
   sauce
5 slices sharp Cheddar
   cheese

Arrange peppers in 8-cup microproof ring mold or 10-inch microproof pie plate. Combine remaining ingredients, except tomato sauce and cheese; blend thoroughly. Divide meat mixture among peppers. Pour tomato sauce over peppers. Cover with plastic wrap. Cook on HI (max. power) 25 to 27 minutes, or until peppers are tender and beef is no longer red. Remove plastic wrap; top each pepper with cheese slice. Return plastic wrap. Let stand 5 minutes before serving.

Barbecued Chuck Roast ——————— 6 to 8 servings

Total Cooking Time: 60 to 65 minutes

1 cup barbecue sauce
½ cup chopped onion
1 clove garlic, minced
1 tablespoon all-purpose
   flour
1 tablespoon beef bouillon
   granules
3 pounds boneless beef
   chuck roast

Cut 1-inch strip from open end of 14 × 20-inch cooking bag; set aside. Combine barbecue sauce, onion, garlic, flour, and bouillon in 2-cup glass measure. Place roast in bag. Spoon sauce mixture evenly over roast. Secure bag with reserved strip. Place bag in square microproof baking dish. Cook on 50 (defrost) 30 minutes; turn bag over. Cook on 50 (defrost) 30 to 35 minutes.

Make barbecued beef sandwiches with leftover roast beef by shredding it, mixing with enough sauce to moisten, and heating in buns.

Super Meat Loaf Ring ⎯⎯⎯⎯⎯ 6 to 8 servings

Total Cooking Time: 21½ to 23½ minutes

2 pounds lean ground beef
2 eggs, slightly beaten
2 slices fresh white bread, crumbed
1 envelope onion soup mix
2 tablespoons milk
1 teaspoon prepared mustard
1 tablespoon minced fresh parsley
1 can (8 ounces) tomato sauce, divided

Topping
1 tablespoon brown sugar
1 tablespoon vinegar

In large bowl, combine all ingredients, except tomato sauce. Add ¼ cup tomato sauce to meat mixture; mix thoroughly. Spoon into 4- or 5-cup ring mold (check yours to be certain it will fit your oven). Cook on HI (max. power) 20 to 22 minutes, rotating every 10 minutes. Meat loaf ring is done when it pulls away from side of mold. Let stand 5 minutes; drain. Invert onto warmed serving platter.

To prepare Topping, mix sugar, remaining tomato sauce, and vinegar in 2-cup glass measure. Cook on HI (max. power) 1½ minutes. Stir. Pour half of sauce over meat loaf ring. Serve remaining sauce as gravy.

As a serving suggestion, fill meat loaf ring with hot vegetables such as Brussels sprouts, chopped broccoli, carrots, peas, etc.

If you prefer, brush ring with soy sauce before and after cooking. Omit Topping.

Super Meatloaf Ring (variation), String Beans (Guide, page 64)→

Pot Roast and Vegetables ———— 4 to 6 servings
Total Cooking Time: 55 to 60 minutes

3 tablespoons all-purpose
   flour
½ teaspoon salt
½ teaspoon dry mustard
½ teaspoon garlic powder
¼ teaspoon freshly ground
   pepper
½ cup catsup
½ cup water
1 tablespoon Worcestershire
   sauce
1 boneless chuck roast
   (3 to 4 pounds),
   fat trimmed
3 medium potatoes, peeled
   and halved
2 medium carrots, cut into
   2-inch pieces
3 small onions, cut in half

Cut 1-inch strip from open end of 14×20-inch cooking bag; reserve strip and set aside. In small bowl, combine flour, salt, mustard, garlic powder, and pepper. Stir in catsup, water, and Worcestershire.

Place roast in bag. Spoon seasoning mixture evenly over roast. Add potatoes, carrots, and onions. Turn bag to distribute liquid. Secure end of bag with reserved strip. Place bag in appropriate size microproof baking dish. Cook on HI (max. power) 20 minutes. Turn bag over. Cook on HI (max. power) 20 minutes. If mixture becomes too dry, add small amount of water. Cook on 75 (simmer) 15 to 20 minutes, or until meat reaches desired doneness and vegetables are tender. Let stand in bag 10 minutes before serving.

Louisiana Pepper Steak ———— 4 servings
Total Cooking Time: 27 minutes

1 pound round steak, cut
   in ¼×1-inch strips
1 can (10¾ ounces) beef
   broth
2 medium green peppers,
   seeded and cut in
   strips
¼ cup water
3 tablespoons cornstarch
1 tablespoon steak sauce
1 medium tomato, cut in
   wedges

In 8-inch round microproof casserole, combine steak and broth. Cook on HI (max. power) 18 minutes, or until steak is tender. Add green pepper. Cover with plastic wrap. Cook on HI (max. power) 6 minutes. Combine water, cornstarch, and steak sauce; stir to dissolve cornstarch. Add to steak and peppers. Arrange tomato wedges on top. Cook on HI (max. power) 3 minutes. Serve over hot cooked rice, if desired.

Simmered Corned Beef _____ 4 to 5 servings
Total Cooking Time: 80 minutes

1 corned beef brisket (1 to
   2½ pounds)
1½ cups water
2 cloves garlic, halved
2 bay leaves
4 peppercorns
1 large onion, sliced

In 2-quart microproof casserole, combine brisket, water, garlic, bay leaves, and peppercorns. Arrange sliced onion over brisket. Cover. Cook on HI (max. power) 30 minutes; turn brisket. Add more water, if necessary. Cover. Cook on 60 (braise) 50 minutes, or until brisket is tender, turning after 25 minutes. Let stand in liquid 15 minutes. Cut in thin slices across the grain.

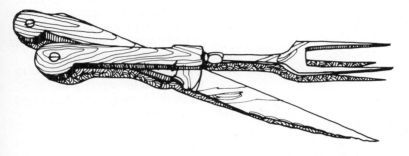

Leftover Meat Stew _____ 5 to 6 servings
Total Cooking Time: 38 to 43 minutes

2 cups cubed beef,
   pork, or lamb
4 medium carrots, peeled
   and sliced
3 medium potatoes, peeled
   and cubed
1 medium onion, quartered
1 cup water
1 package (¾ ounce)
   mushroom gravy mix
1 teaspoon Worcestershire
   sauce
1 teaspoon salt
⅛ teaspoon freshly ground
   pepper
1 cup fresh or frozen peas
   Minced fresh parsley

Combine all ingredients, except peas and parsley, in 2-quart microproof casserole. Cover. Cook on HI (max. power) 35 to 40 minutes, or until vegetables are tender, stirring every 10 minutes. Stir in peas. Cover. Cook on 75 (simmer) 3 minutes. Sprinkle with parsley. Let stand 5 minutes before serving.

The following mixtures can be substituted for the mushroom gravy mix: 1½ cups leftover gravy mixed with ¼ cup water, or 1 can (10¾ ounces) condensed cream of celery soup mixed with ¾ cup water.

Polynesian Pork Kabobs ——————— 4 servings
Total Cooking Time: 9½ minutes

½ cup bottled teriyaki
    marinade
2 tablespoons honey
1 teaspoon vinegar
½ pound pork tenderloin,
    cut into 16 1-inch cubes
1 small green pepper,
    seeded and cut in
    squares
8 large mushrooms, stems
    removed
1 can (8 ounces) pineapple
    chunks, drained
8 cherry tomatoes

In 4-cup glass measure, mix marinade, honey, and vinegar. Add pork cubes; stir to coat. Cover with waxed paper. Cook on HI (max. power) 5 minutes, stirring halfway through cooking time. Set aside to cool. Thread pork, green pepper squares, mushrooms, pineapple chunks, and cherry tomatoes on wooden or bamboo skewers alternately. Repeat with remaining ingredients. Arrange on 10- or 11-inch microproof plate in spoke fashion with tomatoes in center. Brush with marinade.

Cook on HI (max. power) 4½ minutes, or until vegetables are crisp-tender, turning skewers once during cooking time. Cover and let stand 2 minutes. Serve with hot cooked rice seasoned with curry, if desired.

Spareribs in Barbecue Sauce ——————— 4 servings
Total Cooking Time: 35 to 36 minutes

2 pounds lean spareribs,
    cut in serving pieces
1 can (8 ounces) tomato
    sauce
¼ cup firmly packed brown
    sugar
¼ cup cider vinegar
2 tablespoons instant
    minced onion
1 tablespoon horseradish
1 tablespoon Worcestershire
    sauce
1 clove garlic, minced
½ teaspoon salt
½ teaspoon dry mustard
⅛ teaspoon turmeric

Arrange ribs in 2-quart microproof casserole. In small bowl, combine remaining ingredients; blend well. Pour sauce over ribs. Cover. Cook on HI (max. power) 13 minutes; turn ribs. Cover. Cook on HI (max. power) 13 minutes; rearrange ribs. Cover. Cook on 50 (defrost) 9 to 10 minutes, or until ribs are tender. Let stand 3 minutes before serving.

Polynesian Pork Kabobs→

Sauced Pork Chops _____ 4 servings

Total Cooking Time: 25 to 27 minutes

4 center loin pork chops
(about ¾ inch thick)
¼ teaspoon salt
¼ teaspoon freshly ground
pepper
1 can (11 ounces) mandarin
oranges, drained,
liquid reserved
½ cup chopped chutney
2 tablespoons lemon juice
1 tablespoon sugar
1 tablespoon cornstarch

Arrange pork chops in 8-inch round microproof baking dish placing thickest portions toward outside of dish. Sprinkle with salt and pepper. Cover with waxed paper. Cook on HI (max. power) 13 minutes; drain; turn chops over. Mix ⅓ cup reserved orange liquid with chutney, lemon juice, and sugar. Arrange orange sections over pork chops. Top with chutney mixture. Cover. Cook on HI (max. power) 9 to 10 minutes, or until thoroughly done. Remove chops to warmed serving platter. Cover to keep warm.

Mix cornstarch and 2 tablespoons orange liquid. Stir into juices in dish. Cook on HI (max. power) 3 to 4 minutes, or until thickened and smooth, stirring twice during cooking. Spoon over chops.

Sliced Ham with Cherries _____ 6 to 8 servings

Total Cooking Time: 18½ minutes

¼ cup Burgundy
¼ cup firmly packed brown
sugar
2 tablespoons butter or
margarine
¼ teaspoon ginger
¼ teaspoon cloves
1 slice (1½ pounds)
cooked ham
1 cup cherry pie filling

In 11 × 8 × 2-inch oval glass baking dish, mix wine, sugar, butter, ginger and cloves. Cook on HI (max. power) 1½ minutes, or until butter is melted and sugar dissolved. Stir. Add ham; turn to coat. Cover with waxed paper. Cook on HI (max. power) 13 minutes, or until heated through. Rotate dish halfway through cooking time. Remove ham to serving platter. Add cherry pie filling to sauce; stir. Cover. Cook on HI (max. power) 4 minutes, or until thick and heated through. Pour sauce over ham and serve.

If using fresh ham, cook on HI (max. power) 30 minutes.

Veal-Caraway Stew _____ 4 servings

Total Cooking Time: 67 to 77 minutes

1 pound boneless veal, cut
   into 1-inch cubes
1 package (1½ ounces) brown
   gravy mix
1 cup chicken broth
1 teaspoon salt
⅛ teaspoon freshly ground
   pepper
2 tablespoons minced onion
2 stalks celery, sliced
2 medium carrots, thinly
   sliced
2 teaspoons caraway seeds
   Hot cooked noodles or
   spaetzle

In 2-quart microproof casserole, combine veal, gravy mix, and chicken broth. Cover. Cook on HI (max. power) 7 minutes, stirring once during cooking time. Add remaining ingredients, except noodles; blend well. Cover. Cook on 60 (braise) 60 to 70 minutes, or until meat and vegetables are tender, stirring once during cooking time. Let stand 5 minutes before serving with noodles or spaetzle.

A combination of ½ pound pork and ½ pound veal can be substituted for all veal.

Baked Ham Classic _____ 8 to 12 servings

Total Cooking Time: 29 to 30½ minutes

1 canned (3 pounds) ham
   Whole cloves
3 tablespoons brown sugar
2 tablespoons apple or
   orange juice
1 tablespoon cornstarch
1 teaspoon dry mustard

Place ham in microproof baking dish. Cover with waxed paper. Cook on HI (max. power) 15½ minutes. Turn ham over. Score top in diamond pattern. Insert clove in center of each diamond. Combine sugar, juice, cornstarch, and mustard in 2-cup glass measure. Cook on HI (max. power) 1½ minutes, or until thickened. Brush half of glaze over ham. Cook on HI (max. power) 12 to 13½ minutes, or until heated through (120°F on microwave meat thermometer). Reglaze ham after 5 minutes. Let stand, covered with foil, for 15 minutes before serving.

Exotic Lamb Ragout —————————— 4 servings

Total Cooking Time: 68 minutes

1 tablespoon vegetable oil
1 cup chopped onions
1 pound boneless lamb, cut into 1-inch cubes
1 package (1½ ounces) brown gravy mix
2 cups chicken broth, divided
1 teaspoon salt
⅛ teaspoon freshly ground pepper
½ teaspoon nutmeg
½ cup raisins
½ cup long-grain rice
1 tablespoon lemon juice
1 tablespoon butter or margarine
½ cup blanched slivered almonds

In shallow 3-quart microproof casserole, combine oil and onions. Cook on HI (max. power) 5 minutes. Add lamb, gravy mix, and 1 cup of the chicken broth. Cook on HI (max. power) 10 minutes. Stir in salt, pepper, nutmeg, raisins, rice, remaining 1 cup broth, and lemon juice. Cover. Cook on 60 (braise) 45 minutes, or until rice and lamb are tender, stirring every 10 minutes. Add small amount water if mixture becomes dry. Set aside. Place butter in 8-inch glass pie plate. Cook on HI (max. power) 1 minute, or until melted. Stir in almonds. Cover with waxed paper. Cook on HI (max. power) 7 minutes, or until almonds are golden, stirring twice during cooking time. Sprinkle almonds over lamb and serve.

Braised Lamb Shanks —————————— 2 servings

Total Cooking Time: 25½ minutes

2 lamb shanks
1 can (10½ ounces) beef broth
½ teaspoon onion flakes
1 clove garlic, minced
¼ teaspoon freshly ground pepper
1 bay leaf

Place lamb shanks in square microproof baking dish. Combine remaining ingredients; blend well; pour over lamb. Cover with plastic wrap. Cook on 50 (defrost) 10 minutes. Turn lamb over. Cover. Cook on HI (max. power) 15½ minutes, or until lamb is no longer pink. Discard bay leaf. Let stand 5 minutes before serving.

POULTRY PLATTERS

Plain, crumb-coated, soy brushed, barbecue-sauced, and honey-glazed chicken breasts (right). A microwave thermometer takes the guessing out of cooking whole poultry (above).

Still about our most economical food, chicken is more juicy, flavorful, and tender than ever when cooked in the microwave oven. It is a special favorite of microwave cooks because it requires less attention than most main dish meat. Duck and Cornish hen are great, too, as is turkey, though you'll need to select a small turkey that fits in your oven or prepare turkey parts.

Poultry turns out golden brown, though not dark brown or crisp. If you are a crisp-skin lover, the microwave oven is still for you. Simply crisp the skin in a conventional oven at 450°F for 5 or 10 minutes, after the microwave cooking time. And how about this time-saving twist for charcoal grilling: you can avoid the long time delays by partially cooking poultry in the microwave oven, then finishing it on the grill! Full charcoal-grilled flavor is retained. Try our recipes, then adapt your own favorites.

←*Arrange chicken pieces with thickest portions along edge of dish.*

Converting Your Recipes

Conventional one-dish poultry recipes that call for cut-up pieces are easy to adapt for the microwave oven. You are sure to find a similar recipe in this chapter to use as a guide. Here, too, are some tips to follow:

☐ Use care in selecting whole poultry. Chances are your oven will not be able to manage a whole turkey. (Even the largest microwave ovens cannot accommodate a turkey larger than 12 to 14 pounds.)
☐ Conventional pop-up indicators for doneness do not work correctly in the microwave oven.
☐ When using a microwave thermometer, insert it in the fleshy part of the inside thigh muscle, without touching the bone.
☐ Standing time is essential to complete cooking. Allow up to 15 minutes standing time for whole poultry depending upon size. The internal temperature will rise approximately 15°F during 15 minutes standing time. Chicken pieces and casseroles need only 5 minutes standing time.

The Defrosting Guide

1. Remove poultry from its original closed package to ensure even thawing. Remove all metal rings, wire twist ties, and any aluminum foil. The metal leg clamps need not be removed until after defrosting. Be careful, of course, that the metal is at least 1 inch from the oven walls.

2. Place poultry in microproof dish while defrosting.

3. Defrost only as long as necessary. Poultry should be cool in the center when removed from the oven.

4. To speed defrosting during standing time, poultry may be placed in cold water.

5. Separate chicken pieces as soon as partially thawed.

6. Wing and leg tips and area near breastbone may begin cooking before center is thoroughly defrosted. When these areas appear thawed, cover them with small strips of aluminum foil; this foil should be at least 1 inch from oven walls.

DEFROSTING GUIDE — POULTRY

Food	Amount	Minutes (per pound)	Power Control Setting	Standing Time (minutes)	Special Notes
Chicken, cut up	2-3 lbs.	7 - 9	50 (defrost)	10 - 15	Turn every 5 minutes. Separate pieces when partially thawed.
Chicken, whole	2-3 lbs.	6 - 8	50 (defrost)	25 - 30	Turn over once. Immerse in cold water for standing time.
Cornish hens	1, 1-1½ lbs. 2, 1-1½ lbs. each	6 - 8 9 - 11	50 (defrost) 50 (defrost)	20 - 25 20 - 25	Turn over once; remove giblets.
Duckling	4-5 lbs.	9 - 10	50 (defrost)	30 - 40	Turn over once. Immerse in cold water for standing time.
Turkey breast	Under 4 lbs.	3 - 5	50 (defrost)	20 - 30	Turn over once.
Turkey drumsticks	1-1½ lbs.	7 - 9	50 (defrost)	15 - 20	Turn every 5 minutes. Separate pieces when partially thawed.
Turkey roast, boneless	2-4 lbs.	8 - 10	50 (defrost)	10	Remove from foil pan. Cover with waxed paper.

Using the Cooking Guide

1. Defrost frozen poultry completely before cooking.
2. Remove giblets and rinse poultry in cool water, then pat dry.
3. When cooking whole birds, place on a microproof roasting rack in a glass baking dish large enough to catch drippings.
4. Turn over, as directed in Guide, halfway through cooking time.
5. Cook whole poultry covered loosely with a waxed paper tent to prevent splattering. Toward end of cooking time, small pieces of aluminum foil may be used to cover legs, wing tips, or breastbone area to prevent overcooking. Foil should be at least 1 inch from oven walls.
6. Cover poultry pieces with glass lid or plastic wrap during cooking.
7. Standing time completes the cooking of poultry. Cooked whole birds may be covered with aluminum foil during standing time.

COOKING GUIDE — POULTRY
Cook on HI (max. power).

Food	First Cook Time (minutes)	Second Cook Time (minutes)	Standing Time (minutes)	Special Notes
Chicken, whole, 2-3 pounds	7 - 9 per pound	Turn over. 8 - 9 per pound	5 (covered with foil)	Shallow baking dish, roasting rack, breast down.
3-4 pounds	8 - 9 per pound	Turn over.	5	6x9-inch baking dish, roasting rack, breast down.
Chicken, cut up 2½-3½ pounds	7 - 9 per pound	Turn over. 8 - 9 per pound	5	6x9-inch baking dish. Cover.
Chicken, quartered	7 - 9 per pound	Turn over. 8 - 9 per pound	5	Shallow baking dish, skin side down.
Cornish hens 1-1½ pounds	4 - 5 per pound	Turn over. 4 per pound	5	Shallow baking dish, breast down. Cover.
Duckling 4-5 pounds	7 - 8 per pound	Turn over. Drain excess fat. 8 - 9 per pound	8-10	Shallow baking dish, roasting rack. Cover.
Turkey breast, 3-4 pounds	8½ - 9 per pound	Turn over. 5 - 6 per pound		Shallow baking dish, roasting rack.
Turkey roast, boneless 2-4 pounds	10 - 11 per pound	Turn over. 10 per pound	10-15	Loaf pan. Cover with plastic wrap.
Turkey parts, 2-3 pounds	7 - 9 per pound	Turn over. 8 - 9 per pound	5	Shallow baking dish with roasting rack.

West Indian Chicken _____ 6 to 8 servings

Total Cooking Time: 36½ to 38½ minutes

1 tablespoon butter or margarine
6 to 8 chicken thighs, skinned
1 cup minced onion
2 tablespoons lemon juice
1 tablespoon brown sugar
½ teaspoon salt
1 cup chopped tomato
2 tablespoons raisins
1 teaspoon oregano
½ teaspoon thyme
1 teaspoon Worcestershire sauce
2 tablespoons sweet vermouth
2 cups hot cooked rice

Place browning dish in oven. Cook on HI (max. power) 9 minutes. Add butter. When butter is melted, quickly add chicken thighs to brown. Cook on HI (max. power) 3½ minutes. Turn chicken. Add onion and lemon juice; sprinkle sugar and salt over chicken. Cover. Cook on HI (max. power 7 to 9 minutes, or until onion is tender. Add tomato, raisins, oregano, thyme, Worcestershire, and vermouth. Cover. Cook on 50 (defrost) 17 minutes, or until chicken is tender and all ingredients are blended. Serve with rice.

COOKING GUIDE — CONVENIENCE POULTRY

Food	Amount	Power Control Setting	Time (minutes)	Special Notes
Precooked breaded chicken, frozen	1 piece 2 pieces 4 pieces 2-3 lbs	HI (max. power)	1½ - 2½ 2½ - 3½ 3 - 4 14 - 16	Remove wrapping and place in microproof baking dish.
Chicken Kiev, frozen	1 piece 2 pieces	Follow package directions		Remove plastic wrap, place on microproof plate.
Chicken à la King, frozen	5 oz.	Follow package directions		Place on microproof plate. Stir before serving.
Creamed chicken, chicken and dumplings, canned	7½-10½ oz.	HI (max. power)	5 - 7	Stir once.
Escalloped chicken, chow mein, canned	14-24 oz.	HI (max. power)	6 - 8	Stir halfway through cooking time.
Turkey tetrazzini, frozen	12 oz.	HI (max. power)	5 - 7	Place on microproof plate. Stir before serving.
Turkey, sliced in gravy, frozen	5 oz.	HI (max. power)	8 - 10	Place in microproof dish. Make slit in pouch before heating.

Oven Baked Chicken —————— 4 to 6 servings

Total Cooking Time: 31 to 34 minutes

2½ -to 3-pound frying
    chicken, cut up
⅓ cup sherry
1 envelope (2⅜ ounces)
    seasoned coating mix
    for chicken

Wash chicken and pat dry with paper towels. Dip in sherry. Place seasoned coating mix in plastic bag. Shake a few pieces of chicken at a time until coated. Arrange in 10-inch round microproof dish, skin-side up, with thickest portions toward outside of dish. Cover with paper towels. Cook on HI (max. power) 31 to 34 minutes, or until chicken is tender. Let stand 5 minutes before serving.

For crispier and browner chicken, do not cover. If splattering occurs, cover lightly with paper towels.

To reduce calories, substitute chicken bouillon for sherry.

Chicken Tetrazzini _____ 4 to 6 servings

Total Cooking Time: 14½ to 20 minutes

2 ounces uncooked spaghetti, broken into 2-inch pieces
1 tablespoon butter or margarine
⅓ cup minced onion
¼ pound mushrooms, sliced
1½ tablespoons all-purpose flour
1 cup chicken broth
¼ cup light cream or half-and-half
⅛ cup dry vermouth
½ cup grated Parmesan cheese, divided
¼ teaspoon salt
Dash white pepper
1 cup diced cooked chicken
1 tablespoon minced fresh parsley

Cook spaghetti according to package directions. Drain immediately; rinse in cold water to stop cooking; set aside.

In 1½-quart microproof casserole, place butter, onion, and mushrooms. Cover. Cook on HI (max. power) 2½ to 3½ minutes, or until onion is transparent. Stir in flour to make a paste.

In 4-cup glass measure, combine broth, cream, and vermouth. Cook on HI (max. power) 2½ minutes; slowly stir into flour mixture; blend thoroughly. Stir in ¼ cup cheese, salt, and pepper; blend well. Cook on HI (max. power) 7 to 10 minutes, or until mixture comes to a boil and thickens, stirring once during cooking time.

Carefully stir in cooked spaghetti, chicken, and remaining cheese. Cover. Cook on HI (max. power) 2½ to 4 minutes. Let stand, covered, 5 minutes before serving. Sprinkle with parsley.

Chicken Stroganoff _____ 6 servings

Total Cooking Time: 35 to 38 minutes

1 large onion, chopped
1 tablespoon vegetable oil
1 tablespoon prepared mustard
1 can (8 ounces) tomato sauce
1 can (4 ounces) mushroom pieces, drained
3 whole chicken breasts, halved, skinned, and boned
½ cup dairy sour cream
2 tablespoons minced fresh parsley

In 4-cup glass measure, combine onion and oil. Cook on HI (max. power) 6 minutes, or until onion is transparent. Stir in mustard, tomato sauce, and mushrooms; set aside.

Place chicken in shallow 1½-quart microproof casserole; spoon tomato sauce over chicken. Cover with plastic wrap. Cook on HI (max. power) 14 minutes. Rearrange chicken and cook on HI (max. power) 13 to 15 minutes. Use slotted spoon to remove chicken to a warmed serving platter. Stir sour cream into tomato sauce. Cook on 75 (simmer) 2 to 3 minutes, or until hot. Pour over chicken, sprinkle with parsley, and serve. Serve with noodles or rice, if desired.

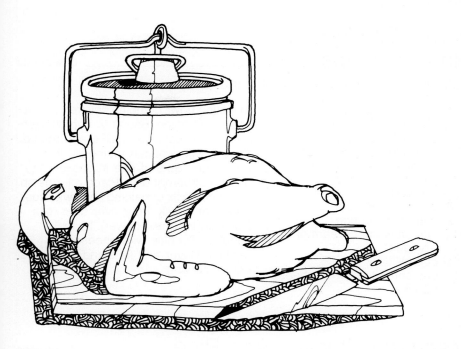

Halved Cornish Hens _____ 4 servings

Total Cooking Time: 22 to 24 minutes

2 Cornish hens (1 pound,
6 ounces each), halved
lengthwise
5 tablespoons dry vermouth,
divided
1 envelope seasoned
coating mix for
chicken
1 teaspoon thyme
4 canned peach halves,
drained

Rinse Cornish hen halves; pat dry with paper towels. Brush on all sides with ¼ cup of the vermouth. Blend coating mix with thyme in a plastic bag. Shake 1 hen half at a time in plastic bag until thoroughly coated.

Arrange halves, skin-side up, with thickest portion toward outside of a 10-inch microproof pie plate. Cover with waxed paper. Cook on HI (max. power) 20 to 22 minutes, or until tender.

Place peach halves, cut-side up, in center of pie plate. Divide remaining vermouth among centers of peaches. Cover with waxed paper. Cook on HI (max. power) 2 minutes, or until peaches are warm.

Cracker or cornflake crumbs can be used in place of seasoned coating mix.

Swiss Chicken and Ham Roll-Ups _____ 6 servings

Total Cooking Time: 12 to 14 minutes

1½ cups coarsely ground
    cooked chicken
1 can (10¾ ounces)
    condensed cream of
    chicken soup, divided
1 green onion, thinly
    sliced
6 slices boiled ham
2 cups cooked rice
¼ cup dairy sour cream or
    yogurt
¼ cup milk
½ cup shredded Swiss cheese
    Paprika

In mixing bowl, combine chicken, ⅓ cup soup, and onion. Spoon ¼ cup chicken mixture on each ham slice and roll up. Secure with wooden toothpick, if necessary. Spread rice in shallow 1½-quart microproof dish. Place roll-ups on top of rice. Mix remaining soup with sour cream and milk. Pour over ham rolls. Cook on HI (max. power) 12 to 14 minutes. Sprinkle with cheese and paprika. Cover and let stand 5 minutes before serving.

Mandarin Chicken and Rice _____ 4 servings

Total Cooking Time: 26 minutes

1 can (16 ounces) chop suey
    vegetables, drained
1 can (10¾ ounces)
    condensed cream of
    mushroom soup
¾ cup quick-cooking rice
1 can (5.3 ounces)
    evaporated milk
1 can (4 ounces) mushroom
    pieces, undrained
¼ cup minced onion
2 whole chicken breasts,
    boned and halved
    Paprika

In 3-quart microproof casserole, blend vegetables, soup, rice, milk, mushrooms with liquid, and onion. Cover. Cook on HI (max. power) 6 minutes, stirring halfway through cooking time. Arrange chicken breasts on top of casserole, placing thickest parts toward outside of casserole. Cover. Cook on HI (max. power) 20 minutes, or until tender. Sprinkle with paprika. Let stand, covered, 5 minutes before serving.

Mandarin Chicken and Rice, Swiss Chicken and Ham Roll-Ups →

Micro-Fried Chicken Steaks _____ 4 patties

Total Cooking Time: 14 to 16 minutes

1½ cups fresh bread crumbs,
    divided
1 cup cooked chicken,
    chopped
⅓ cup milk
2 tablespoons chopped onion
1 tablespoon minced fresh
    parsley
¼ teaspoon salt
⅛ teaspoon pepper
½ teaspoon paprika
    White Sauce (page 73)

In a 1½-quart bowl, combine 1 cup bread crumbs, chicken, milk, onion, parsley, salt, and pepper. Form into 4 patties. Mix paprika with remaining bread crumbs. Coat patties with crumb mixture. Place on 9-inch microproof plate. Cook on HI (max. power) 3½ minutes; turn patties over and continue to cook 2½ to 3½ minutes. Top with White Sauce. Sprinkle with remaining bread crumbs.

Chicken Breasts with Cashews _____ 4 servings

Total Cooking Time: 28½ to 32½ minutes

1 package (6 ounces) frozen
    pea pods
2 tablespoons dry white wine
    or water
1 tablespoon soy sauce
1 tablespoon oil
1 tablespoon cornstarch
⅛ teaspoon pepper
⅛ teaspoon hot sauce
2 whole boneless chicken
    breasts, skinned
    and flattened to
    ¼-inch thickness
1 medium onion, sliced into
    rings
1 red or green pepper,
    sliced into strips
2 tablespoons oil
1 cup whole cashews,
    unsalted
½ cup chicken stock or
    bouillon

Cook pea pods on 50 (defrost) 4½ minutes. Set aside. In a small bowl, combine wine, soy sauce, oil, cornstarch, pepper, and hot sauce. Cut each whole chicken breast into 4 to 6 pieces. Add each piece to wine marinade, then place chicken in a 9- or 10-inch microproof pie plate. Pour remaining marinade over pieces; allow to marinate 15 to 20 minutes. In a 2-quart microproof bowl, combine onion, pepper slices, and oil. Cook on HI (max. power) 6 to 7 minutes, stirring once. Add cashews and chicken stock. Pour marinade into onion-oil mixture. Stir to blend well. Cook chicken pieces on HI (max. power) 4 minutes. Turn pieces over and rearrange. Cook on HI (max. power) 4 to 5 minutes, or until chicken loses its pink color. Cover and set aside. Cook sauce mixture on HI (max. power), covered, 6 to 7 minutes, or until thickened. Stir in pea pods. Spoon sauce over chicken. Cook on HI (max. power) 4 to 5 minutes, or until heated through. Serve over hot cooked rice.

Wagonwheel Drumsticks Dinner ___ 2 servings

Total Cooking Time: 25 to 27 minutes

4 chicken legs (about
   1 pound)
2 tablespoons Italian salad
   dressing
¼ cup Italian seasoned
   bread crumbs
2 8-ounce potatoes, cut in
   half lengthwise
2 tablespoons butter, melted
¼ cup Parmesan cheese
   Paprika

Coat chicken legs with Italian dressing and bread crumbs. Place in a 10-inch round microproof plate in spoke fashion, with meaty portion of leg on the outer edges. Place a potato half between each leg, skin-side down. Brush with butter and Parmesan cheese. Sprinkle with paprika. Cover with paper towel. Cook on HI (max. power) 13 minutes, rotating dish once. Turn legs over and turn potatoes around. Cook on HI (max. power) 12 to 14 minutes, or until legs are done, rotating dish once.

Stuffed Whole Chicken _____ 2 servings

Total Cooking Time: 34 to 40 minutes

1 2½-3-pound whole
    broiler-fryer chicken
½ teaspoon salt
    Bread Stuffing (below)
1 clove garlic, halved
1 tablespoon browning
    sauce

Remove giblets and neck from cavity. Rinse chicken and pat dry with paper towels. Rub inside with salt. Fill with stuffing; close opening with toothpicks or wood skewers. Rub skin with cut sides of garlic. Secure legs with string. Mix 2 tablespoons water with browning sauce; brush mixture over chicken. Place, breast side up, in microproof baking dish. Cook on HI, (max. power) 17 minutes. Turn chicken breast side down. Brush drippings over chicken. Cook on HI (max. power) 17 to 23 minutes, or until tender (180°F if using microwave food thermometer). Let stand 10 minutes before serving.

Bread Stuffing _____ 2 servings

Total Cooking Time: 2½ minutes

2 tablespoons butter or
    margarine
2 tablespoons chopped onion
2 tablespoons chopped celery
1½ cups dry bread cubes
½ cup chicken broth or
    water
1 teaspoon chopped parsley
¼ teaspoon salt
⅛ teaspoon freshly ground
    pepper

Combine butter, onion, and celery in 2-cup glass measure. Cook on HI (max. power) 2½ minutes, or until onion is transparent. Stir in remaining ingredients. Makes enough stuffing for 2½- to 3-pound broiler-fryer chicken.

←*Stuffed Whole Chicken*

Brunswick Stew _____ 4 to 6 servings
Total Cooking Time: 26 to 30 minutes

2¼ cups water, divided
2 cups cubed, uncooked chicken
2 chicken bouillon cubes
1 teaspoon parsley flakes
4 peppercorns
1 cup thinly sliced carrots
¼ cup sliced celery
1 medium onion, diced
5 medium mushrooms, sliced (about ½ cup)
3 tablespoons cornstarch

In 2-quart microproof bowl, combine 2 cups water, chicken, bouillon, parsley, and peppercorns. Cook on HI (max. power) 13 minutes. Add carrots, celery, onion, and mushrooms; mix lightly. Combine ¼ cup water and cornstarch; stir to dissolve cornstarch. Add to chicken and vegetables. Cover with plastic wrap. Cook on HI (max. power) 13 to 17 minutes, or until vegetables are tender. Let stand, covered, 10 minutes before serving.

Chicken Liver Chow Mein _____ 4 to 6 servings
Total Cooking Time: 21 to 24 minutes

½ pound chicken livers, rinsed and drained
3 tablespoons butter or margarine, divided
½ cup sliced celery
¼ cup chopped onion
1 envelope (1¾ ounces) mushroom gravy mix
1 can (16 ounces) Chinese vegetables
1 can (8 ounces) sliced water chestnuts, drained
1 tablespoon soy sauce
2 cups cooked rice
Chow mein noodles

Pierce chicken livers in several places with a toothpick. Combine livers with 2 tablespoons of the butter in 4-cup glass measure. Cover. Cook on HI (max. power) 6 to 8 minutes, or until livers are no longer pink, stirring once during cooking time. Drain and set aside.

In 2-quart microproof casserole, mix remaining 1 tablespoon butter with celery and onion. Cover. Cook on HI (max. power) 5 minutes, or until onion is transparent. Stir in gravy mix. Add Chinese vegetables, water chestnuts, and soy sauce; stir lightly. Cover. Cook on HI (max. power) 7 minutes, or until heated through. Cut livers into bite-size pieces. Add to vegetables, stirring carefully. Cook on HI (max. power) 3 to 4 minutes. Let stand covered 5 minutes. Serve over rice. Sprinkle with chow mein noodles.

Turkey Crunch _____ 6 servings

Total Cooking Time: 19 to 21 minutes

1 tablespoon butter or
    margarine
¼ cup sliced celery
¼ cup chopped onion
¼ cup chopped green pepper
1 can (10¾ ounces)
    condensed cream of
    mushroom soup
¼ cup milk
1 can (5 ounces) chow mein
    noodles
1½ cups diced cooked turkey
    or chicken
1 can (4 ounces) mushroom
    pieces, drained
2 tablespoons sliced
    pimiento
¼ teaspoon poultry
    seasoning
¼ teaspoon salt

Combine butter, celery, onion, and green pepper in 2-quart microproof casserole. Cook on HI (max. power) 8 minutes, or until vegetables are tender, stirring once during cooking time. In small bowl, combine soup and milk; stir into onion mixture. Stir in 2 cups chow mein noodles, turkey, mushrooms, pimiento, poultry seasoning, and salt. Cook on HI (max. power) 10 to 12 minutes. Stir. Sprinkle remaining noodles around edges of casserole. Cook on HI (max. power) 1 minute. Let stand 2 minutes before serving.

Glazed Turkey Legs _____ 2 to 4 servings

Total Cooking Time: 34½ to 35 minutes

2 turkey legs (2½ to 3
    pounds)
⅓ cup honey
1 teaspoon grated lemon peel
1 teaspoon lemon juice
1 teaspoon cornstarch
¼ teaspoon bottled brown
    sauce

Place turkey legs in 10-inch round microproof dish; cover with paper towel. Cook on HI (max. power) 14 minutes, turning once. Turn legs over. Cook on HI (max. power) 14 minutes. In a small bowl, combine honey, lemon peel, lemon juice, cornstarch, and brown sauce. Cook on HI (max. power) 1½ to 2 minutes, or until thick. Brush turkey legs with half of the glaze. Cook on HI (max. power) 2½ minutes. Turn legs over; brush with remaining glaze. Cook on HI (max. power) 2½ minutes.

Orange-Glazed Duckling ———————— 4 servings

Total Cooking Time: 59½ to 60 minutes

1 duckling (3 to 4 pounds),
   quartered
Salt and freshly
   ground pepper
¾ cup fresh orange juice
2 tablespoons sugar
2 teaspoons cornstarch
1 tablespoon grated fresh
   orange peel
½ teaspoon garlic powder
1 small orange, sectioned
   and each section
   quartered
2 tablespoons dry sherry

Sprinkle both sides of duckling with salt and pepper. Pierce skin in several places with fork. Place, skin-side up, in shallow oval microproof baking dish with thickest portions toward outside of dish. Cover with waxed paper. Cook on HI (max. power) 30 minutes, covering wings with 1-inch strip of aluminum foil halfway through cooking time. Drain; rearrange pieces, skin-side down. Cover. Cook on HI (max. power) 10 minutes. Turn pieces skin-side up. Cover. Cook on 50 (defrost) 15 minutes, or until tender.

Combine juice, sugar, cornstarch, orange peel, and garlic powder in 2-cup glass measure. Cook on HI (max. power) 4½ to 5 minutes, or until thickened, stirring every minute. Stir in orange sections and sherry. Arrange duck on serving platter. Pour half of sauce over duck. Pass remaining sauce.

SEAFOOD SAMPLER

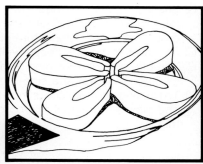

Fish fillets cook best when rolled and arranged around the outside of the dish (left). Fish steaks are arranged as close to a round pattern as possible (above).

In microwave cooking, there's fast and then there's *fast* — seafood cooking. If you have been impressed with the cooking speed of your oven for chicken and other food, you'll be amazed at its performance with fish. For best results, have everything ready and then cook your fish last. Even standing time is short.

Seafood from the microwave oven is a quality success, too. It is so moist, tender, and delicious that you'll never want to cook it any other way. The results are truly as good as if the most accomplished French chef had paid a visit to your kitchen!

Keep in mind that fish is versatile. Most recipes that specify a particular variety will work with many substitutes. When a recipe calls for fish fillets, you can use sole, flounder, bluefish, cod, scrod, perch, or any similar fish. The number one rule in cooking fish: it's done when opaque and barely able to flake.

Converting Your Recipes

As in conventional cooking, the secret to seafood in the microwave oven is to watch it carefully, since fish can overcook in seconds. Other than that, all you need is to refer to a recipe here similar to yours, or find clues in the Guides and these tips:

☐ Cook fish covered unless it is coated with crumbs, which seal in the juices.
☐ When cooking whole fish, the dish should be rotated one-quarter turn twice during the cooking process to help provide even cooking. The odd shape of the fish requires this procedure.
☐ Shellfish is done when flesh is opaque and just firm.
☐ Shellfish come in their own cooking containers which respond well to microwave cooking. Clam and mussel shells open before your eyes. Shrimp, crab, and lobster shells turn pink.
☐ All seafood recipes freeze well except where otherwise noted.
☐ You can use the browning dish for fillets or fish patties. Preheat, add butter or oil, and brown on one side for best results.
☐ To remove seafood odors from the oven, combine 1 cup water with lemon juice and cloves in a small microproof bowl. Use HI (max. power) and cook 6 to 8 minutes.

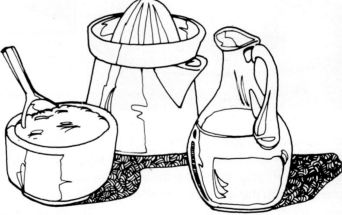

Using the Defrosting Guide

1. Remove fish from its original wrapper for more even thawing. Discard any aluminum foil, metal rings, or wire twist ties.
2. Place fish on microproof dish.
3. To prevent the outer edges from drying out or beginning to cook, it is best to remove fish from oven before it has completely thawed.
4. Finish defrosting under cold running water, separating fillets.

DEFROSTING GUIDE — SEAFOOD

Food	Amount	Control	Time (minutes)	Standing Time (minutes)	Special Notes
Fish fillets	1 lb.	50 (defrost)	9 - 11	5	Defrost on dish.
	2 lbs.	50 (defrost)	13 - 17	5	Carefully separate fillets under cold water. Turn once.
Fish steaks	1 lb.	50 (defrost)	9 - 11	5	Defrost on dish. Carefully separate steaks under cold running water.
Whole fish	8 - 10 oz.	50 (defrost)	6 - 8	5	Shallow dish; shape of fish determines size. Should be icy when removed. Finish at room temperature. Cover head with aluminum foil. Turn once.
	1½ - 2 lbs.	50 (defrost)	7 - 9	5	
Lobster tails	8 oz. package	50 (defrost)	5 - 7	5	Remove from package to baking dish.
Crab legs	8 - 10 oz.	50 (defrost)	5 - 7	5	Glass baking dish. Break apart and turn once.
Crab meat	6 oz.	50 (defrost)	4 - 5	5	Defrost on dish. Break apart. Turn once.
Shrimp	1 lb.	50 (defrost)	6 - 7	5	Remove from package to dish. Spread loosely in baking dish and rearrange during thawing as necessary.
Scallops	1 lb.	50 (defrost)	7 - 10	5	Defrost on dish; spread out on baking dish if in pieces. Turn over and rearrange during thawing as necessary.
Oysters	12 oz.	50 (defrost)	4 - 5	5	Remove from package to dish. Turn over and rearrange during thawing as necessary.

Using the Cooking Guide

1. Defrost seafood fully; then cook.
2. Remove original wrapping Rinse under cold running water.
3. Place seafood in microproof baking dish with thick edges of fillets and steaks and thick ends of shellfish toward the outer edge of the dish.
4. Cover dish with plastic wrap or waxed paper.
5. Test often during the cooking period to avoid overcooking.
6. Method and time are the same for seafood with or without the shell.

COOKING GUIDE — SEAFOOD
Cook on HI (max. power).

Food	Time (minutes)	Standing Time (minutes)	Special Notes
Fish fillets, 1 lb. 2 lbs.	5 - 7 9 - 10	4 - 5 4 - 5	6 × 9 -inch dish, covered.
Fish steaks, 1 inch thick, 1 lb.	10 - 12	5 - 6	6 × 9 -inch dish, covered.
Whole fish 8 - 10 oz. 1½ - 2 lbs.	4 - 5 8 - 10	3 - 4 5	Appropriate shallow dish.
Crab legs 8 - 10 oz. 16 - 20 oz.	4 - 6 7 - 8	5 5	Appropriate shallow dish, covered. Turn once.
Shrimp, scallops 8 oz. 1 lb.	5 - 6 7 - 8		Appropriate shallow dish, covered. Rearrange halfway.
Snails, clams, oysters, 12 oz.	5 - 7		Shallow dish, covered. Rearrange halfway.
Lobster tails 1: 8 oz. 2: 8 oz. each 4: 8 oz. each	4 - 5 7 - 8 12 - 14	5 5 5	Shallow dish. Split shell to reduce curling.

COOKING/DEFROSTING GUIDE — CONVENIENCE SEAFOOD
Cook on HI (max. power).

Food	Amount	Time (minutes)	Special Notes
Shrimp croquettes	12 oz. package	7 - 10	Pierce sauce pouch, place on serving plate with croquettes. Cover, turn halfway through cooking time.
Fish sticks, frozen	4 oz. 8 oz.	3 - 3½ 5 - 6	Will not crisp. Cook on serving plate.
Tuna casserole, frozen	11 oz. package	8 - 12	Remove from package to 1-quart casserole. Stir once during cooking and before serving.
Fish newburg frozen pouch	6½ - 8 oz.	6 - 8	Place pouch on plate. Pierce pouch. Flex pouch to mix halfway through cooking time. Stir before serving.

Fish Fillets Amandine _____ 4 servings

Total Cooking Time: 14½ to 17½ minutes

⅓ cup sliced or slivered
    almonds
¼ cup butter or margarine
1 pound fish fillets, cut
    in serving pieces
½ teaspoon salt
½ teaspoon lemon pepper

Place almonds and butter in 1½-quart round microproof baking dish. Cook on HI (max. power) 6 to 7 minutes, or until almonds are golden, stirring once during cooking time. Remove almonds with slotted spoon; set aside. Add fish fillets; turn to coat both sides. Cover with plastic wrap. Cook on HI (max. power) 8½ to 10½ minutes, or until fish flakes easily and is opaque. Sprinkle with salt, lemon, pepper, and almonds. Cover and let stand 2 minutes before serving.

Poached Fish _____ 4 servings

Total Cooking Time: 25 to 29 minutes

4 cups water
1 cup white wine
1 stalk celery with
    leaves, cut up
1 small onion, sliced
4 lemon slices
1½ teaspoons salt
5 peppercorns
    Fresh parsley
4 fish steaks (¾-to 1-inch
    thick), such as
    halibut or salmon

Combine all ingredients, except fish, in 2-quart microproof casserole. Cover. Cook on HI (max. power) 19 to 22 minutes, or until boiling. Strain liquid; return to casserole. Add fish; spoon liquid over top. Cover. Cook on HI (max. power) 6 to 7 minutes (4 to 5 minutes per pound), or until fish flakes easily and is opaque. (To keep fish from becoming tough, do not overcook.) Let stand 3 minutes in liquid. Remove from liquid and place on serving platter.

Other liquids can be used for poaching, such as clam juice, chicken broth, or tomato juice.

Halibut and Vegetables ——————— 2 servings

Total Cooking Time: 18 to 22 minutes

2 halibut steaks (6 to 8 ounces each) or similar fish
2 medium carrots, split lengthwise and in 2-inch strips
1 small onion, chopped
1 medium potato, peeled and cut in 2-inch strips
1 stalk celery, cut in 2-inch strips
½ green pepper, cut in 2-inch strips
1 small zucchini, split lengthwise and then cut in 2-inch strips
1 tablespoon minced fresh parsley
2 tablespoons butter or margarine
Salt and freshly ground pepper
Paprika

Rinse fish steaks; pat dry with paper towels; set aside. Combine vegetables in shallow 1-quart microproof bowl. Dot with butter. Sprinkle with salt and pepper. Cover with plastic wrap. Cook on HI (max. power) 8 to 10 minutes, or until vegetables are almost tender; stir. Sprinkle with parsley. Arrange fish over vegetables, covering vegetables completely. Season lightly with salt, pepper, and paprika. Cover with plastic wrap. Cook on HI (max. power) 10 to 12 minutes, or until fish flakes easily and is opaque. Let stand, covered, 3 minutes before serving.

Tuna-Zucchini Medley _____ 4 to 6 servings
Total Cooking Time: 21 to 25 minutes

1½ pounds zucchini, rinsed
   and sliced (about
   4 cups)
¼ cup water
1 can (7 ounces) tuna,
   drained and flaked
2 eggs, slightly beaten
1 cup fine bread crumbs,
   divided
1 teaspoon salt
½ teaspoon lemon pepper
2 tablespoons butter or
   margarine

Place zucchini in 2-quart microproof casserole. Add water. Cover. Cook on HI (max. power) 9 to 10 minutes, or until crisp-tender, stirring once during cooking time. Drain. Add tuna, eggs, ½ cup of the bread crumbs, salt, and lemon pepper; mix carefully; set aside.

In 1-cup glass measure, combine butter and remaining ½ cup bread crumbs. Cook on 50 (defrost) 2 minutes; stir. Sprinkle crumbs over casserole. Cook on HI (max. power) 10 to 13 minutes, or until center is set, rotating once during cooking time. Let stand, covered, 5 minutes before serving.

Lemon-Buttered Cod Fillets _____ 4 servings
Total Cooking Time: 8½ to 10½ minutes

1 pound cod fillets
2 tablespoons butter or
   margarine
2 tablespoons lemon juice
½ teaspoon lemon pepper
½ teaspoon salt
  Paprika

Arrange fillets in shallow 1½-quart oval microproof casserole or glass pie plate. Dot with butter. Sprinkle with remaining ingredients. Cover with plastic wrap. Cook on HI (max. power) 8½ to 10½ minutes, or until fish flakes easily and is opaque. Let stand 2 minutes before serving.

Salmon Ring ———————————— 6 to 8 servings

Total Cooking Time: 12 to 14 minutes

1 can (1 pound) red salmon,
   undrained
2 eggs, beaten
1 cup fresh bread crumbs
¼ cup chopped dill pickle
3 tablespoons minced green
   onion
2 tablespoons mayonnaise
¼ teaspoon salt
⅛ teaspoon freshly ground
   pepper
   Parslied Potatoes (page 74)
   Minced fresh parsley

Grease 4-cup microproof ring mold. In large bowl, combine all ingredients, except potatoes and parsley; blend well. Turn into prepared mold, spreading evenly. Cover. Cook on HI (max. power) 12 to 14 minutes, turning once during cooking time. Invert onto serving platter. Fill center of ring with potatoes. Sprinkle with parsley.

Use your imagination in choosing other fillings for this attractive ring. Broccoli, creamed peas and carrots, pearl onions, Brussels sprouts, or rice are our suggestions. You might also simply serve this Salmon Ring with White Sauce (page 73).

Salmon Ring, Broccoli and Sour Cream (page 73), Parslied Potatoes (page 74) →

Salmon Steak
with Cucumber Sauce _____ 2 servings

Total Cooking Time: 8½ to 9½ minutes

¼ cup finely chopped, peeled
    and seeded cucumber
2 tablespoons mayonnaise
2 tablespoons dairy sour
    cream
½ teaspoon chopped chives
    or ¼ teaspoon
    freeze-dried chives
½ teaspoon onion
    flakes
⅛ teaspoon salt
2 salmon steaks (1-inch
    thick)
    Lemon pepper

In small bowl combine cucumber, mayonnaise, sour cream, chives, onion flakes, and salt; set aside.

Place salmon in 2 microproof au gratin dishes or 1 8-inch microproof pie plate. Sprinkle with lemon pepper. Cover with plastic wrap. Cook on HI (max. power) 7 to 8 minutes, or until fish flakes easily and is opaque. Rotate dish once during cooking time. Drain, if necessary.

Spoon cucumber sauce over salmon. Cook on 35 (low) 1½ minutes, or until sauce is warm. Let stand 2 minutes before serving.

To prepare 4 salmon steaks, prepare cucumber sauce, doubling ingredients. Arrange salmon steaks in 10-inch round microproof dish with narrow ends in center. Cook on HI (max. power) 12 to 15 minutes. Spoon Cucumber Sauce over salmon. Cook on 35 (low) 5 to 6 minutes, or until sauce is warm.

To reduce calories, omit the sauce and serve with lemon wedges and minced fresh parsley.

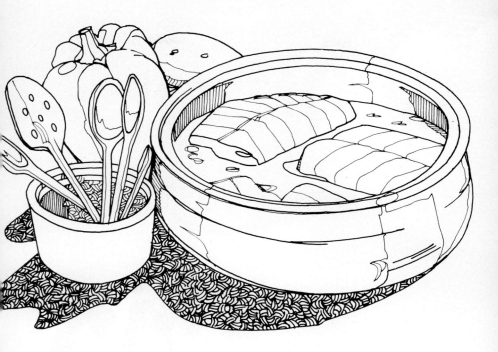

Hawaiian Baked Fish _____ 4 to 6 servings

Total Cooking Time: 13 to 15 minutes

1 cup pineapple juice
2 tablespoons lemon juice
2 tablespoons butter or
    margarine
1 tablespoon minced pimiento
1 tablespoon instant minced
    onion
1½ teaspoons cornstarch
1 teaspoon parsley flakes
½ teaspoon curry powder
2 cups cooked rice
1 pound fresh or thawed
    frozen fish fillets

In 2-cup glass measure, combine pineapple juice, lemon juice, butter, pimiento, onion, cornstarch, parsley, and curry powder; blend well. Cook on HI (max. power) 6 to 7 minutes, or until mixture begins to thicken, stirring twice during cooking time.

Spread rice in shallow 1½-quart microproof casserole. Roll up fillets and place on top of rice. Pour sauce over all. Cover with plastic wrap. Cook on HI (max. power) 7 to 8 minutes, or until fish flakes easily and is opaque. Let stand, covered, 3 minutes, before serving. Garnish with pineapple, if desired.

Herb-Crumbed Fish Fillets ——————— 2 servings

Total Cooking Time: 5 to 6 minutes

4 fish fillets (½ pound)
⅓ cup seasoned Italian
    bread crumbs
¼ cup grated Parmesan cheese
¼ teaspoon garlic powder
¼ teaspoon salt
1 egg white, slightly
    beaten

Rinse fillets; pat dry with paper towels; set aside. In small bowl, combine crumbs, cheese, garlic powder, and salt. Dip fillets in egg white, then in crumb mixture; coat well. Arrange fillets in shallow microproof baking dish, placing thickest part of fillet toward outside of dish. Cover with paper towel. Cook on HI (max. power) 5 to 6 minutes, or until fish flakes easily. Let stand 2 minutes. Serve with lemon wedges.

Poor Man's Lobster ——————— 4 servings

Total Cooking Time: 14½ to 16½ minutes

1 pound cod, boned and cut
    in bite-size pieces
2 cups water
2 tablespoons onion flakes
1 stalk celery, sliced
1 bay leaf
½ teaspoon salt
4 peppercorns
1 cup butter or margarine
¼ cup lemon juice

Combine all ingredients, except butter and lemon juice, in 2-quart microproof bowl. Cook on HI (max. power) 12 to 13 minutes, or until fish flakes easily and is opaque, stirring once during cooking time. Let stand 5 minutes. While fish is standing, combine butter and lemon juice in 2-cup glass measure. Cook on HI (max. power) 2½ to 3½ minutes. Remove cod from cooking broth with a slotted spoon; place on serving platter. Serve with lemon butter for dipping.

←Herb-Crumbed Fish Fillets

Baked Stuffed Fish Fillets _____ 6 servings

Total Cooking Time: 14½ to 17½ minutes

2 tablespoons butter or
   margarine
2 tablespoons minced green
   onion
½ cup bread crumbs
⅔ cup chopped mushrooms
2 pounds flounder or
   sole fillets
   White Sauce (page 73)
¼ cup white wine
½ cup shredded Swiss
   cheese
1 teaspoon chopped fresh
   parsley
½ teaspoon paprika

Combine butter, onion, and mushrooms in 4-cup glass measure. Cook on HI (max. power) 2½ minutes, or until onion is transparent; mix in bread crumbs. Rinse and pat dry fillets. Divide crumb mixture onto each fillet. Roll fillets; place, seam-side down, in 6 × 9-inch microproof baking dish; set aside. Prepare White Sauce. When thick and hot, stir in cheese until melted. Stir in wine and pour over fish. Cover with plastic wrap. Cook on HI (max. power) 12 to 15 minutes, or until fish is opaque. Sprinkle with parsley and paprika. Serve hot.

Clams with Creamy Garlic Sauce _____ 4 servings

Total Cooking Time: 18 to 20 minutes

24 clams in the shell,
   well scrubbed

Sauce

2 tablespoons onion, finely
   minced
1 clove garlic, finely minced
2 tablespoons dry white wine
¼ teaspoon salt
⅛ teaspoon pepper
½ cup butter, chilled and
   cut into 8 pieces

Arrange half the clams in a circle on a microproof plate with hinges toward rim. Cook on HI (max. power) 7 to 8 minutes, or until shells open. Remove as soon as they open. Repeat with remaining shells. Break off top shell and arrange in a circle on plate. Cover with plastic wrap. Set aside.

In a 4-cup glass measure, combine onion, garlic, wine, salt, and pepper. Cook on HI (max. power) 3 minutes. Quickly whisk in butter, 1 tablespoon at a time. Return to oven. Cook on HI (max. power) for 1 minute after 2 tablespoons butter are added. The sauce should be creamy and slightly thickened. Spoon butter sauce on each clam. Serve hot.

Poached Oysters _____ 4 to 6 servings

Total Cooking Time: 7 to 9½ minutes

2 tablespoons butter
2 tablespoons flour
⅛ teaspoon white pepper
1 pint oysters, drained, reserve liquid
1 cup oyster liquid and milk to equal 1 cup
½ teaspoon Worcestershire sauce
½ teaspoon lemon juice
Buttered toast tips
Paprika or cayenne pepper
Minced fresh parsley

Place butter in 4-cup glass measure. Cook on HI (max. power) 30 to 45 seconds, or until butter is melted. Stir in flour. Cook on HI (max. power) 30 to 45 seconds. Briskly stir in oyster liquid and milk mixture. Cook on HI (max. power) 4 to 5 minutes, or until thickened. Stir in oysters, Worcestershire, and lemon juice. Cook on 50 (defrost) 2 to 3 minutes, stirring once. Serve on toast tips. Sprinkle with paprika and parsley.

Shrimp Newburg _____ 4 servings

Total Cooking Time: 14 to 17½ minutes

¼ cup butter or margarine
¼ cup chopped onion
2 tablespoons all-purpose flour
½ teaspoon salt
1½ cups milk
2 egg yolks, beaten
1 teaspoon grated lemon rind
1 package (8 to 12 ounces) frozen cooked shrimp, thawed
1 can (4 ounces) sliced mushrooms, drained

Combine butter and onion in 2-quart microproof casserole. Cook on HI (max. power) 2½ to 3½ minutes, or until onion is transparent. Stir in flour and salt. Cook on HI (max. power) 1 minute. Pour milk into 2-cup glass measure. Cook on HI (max. power) 2½ minutes, or until warm. Stir into flour mixture; blend until smooth. Cook on HI (max. power) 3½ to 4 minutes, stirring once during cooking time. Stir small amount into egg yolks; then pour egg mixture back into sauce; blend well. Stir in lemon rind. Cook on 50 (defrost) 2½ to 3½ minutes, or until thickened and hot, stirring every 2 minutes. Stir in shrimp and mushrooms. Cook on 50 (defrost) 2 to 3½ minutes. Serve over rice or toast points.

To substitute fresh mushrooms for canned, combine with onion and butter. Cook on HI (max. power) 6 to 8 minutes.

Jambalaya ——————————————— 4 servings

Total Cooking Time: 10 to 15 minutes

2 slices bacon, cut into
  pieces
1 can (10¾ ounces)
  tomato purée
1 can (4½ ounces) large
  shrimp, drained
1 cup water
1 cup quick-cooking rice
1 teaspoon onion flakes
1 teaspoon parsley flakes
½ teaspoon Worcestershire
  sauce
¼ teaspoon thyme

Place bacon in 2-quart microproof casserole. Cook on HI (max. power) 2 minutes; drain. Add remaining ingredients; stir to blend. Cook on HI (max. power) 8 to 13 minutes, or until rice is tender. Let stand 3 minutes before serving.

HOME BAKED GOODNESS

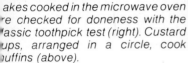

akes cooked in the microwave oven
re checked for doneness with the
'assic toothpick test (right). Custard
ups, arranged in a circle, cook
uffins (above).

Treat your family and friends to the rich aroma of a hot-from-the-oven homemade bread. For a quick and easy surprise breakfast, or as a coffee-klatch companion, you can count on baked goods from the microwave oven.

All baked goods have excellent texture, but they do not brown or develop crust. There is no hot air to dry the surface as in conventional baking. For this reason, most microwave recipes call for dark flours, or add molasses and spices. The absent crust is a benefit, however, enabling much higher rising of cakes and bread. For this reason, larger loaf pans are often recommended. It's also beneficial to use ring molds or bundt-type microproof pans for more even cooking.

Are there any chocolate-covered-cherries fans at your house? If so, you'll want to start off with Chocolate Cherry Bundt Cake (page 152). Pecan Rum Pie (page 150), too, is a can't-wait-to-try treat.

Converting Your Recipes

When adapting "quick bread" recipes, you will find it necessary to reduce the amount of leavening (baking powder or soda) by about one-quarter the normal amount. A bitter aftertaste is apparent if too much leavening is used in biscuits or muffins. Since food rises higher in the microwave oven, you will not see a loss in volume from the reduction of soda or baking powder. If a recipe contains buttermilk or sour cream, do not change the amount of soda, since it serves to counteract the sour taste and does not act only as a leavening agent. When using a mix where leavening cannot be reduced, if you allow the dough to stand about 10 minutes before cooking, some of the gas will be lost. And observe the following tips:

☐ Fill paper-lined muffin cups only half full to allow for muffins rising more.
☐ You can prepare your own "brown 'n serve" breads and rolls by baking them ahead in the microwave oven. Then place them in the conventional oven to brown just before serving.
☐ Breads and rolls should be reheated to the point where they are warm to the touch. Overheating or overcooking makes bread tough and rubbery.
☐ When making yeast bread in a microwave oven, choose a recipe with cornmeal, whole wheat flour, or rye flour to achieve a rich color.

COOKING GUIDE — PUDDING AND PIE FILLING MIX

Food	Amount	Time (minutes)	Power Control Setting	Special Notes
Pudding and pie filling mix	3¼ ounces	8 - 10	HI (max. power)	Follow package directions.
	5½ ounces	15 - 17	HI (max. power)	Stir every 3 minutes. Use 4-cup glass measure.
Egg custard	3 ounces	8 - 11	HI (max. power)	Follow package directions. Stir every 3 minutes. Use 4-cup glass measure.
Tapioca	3¼ ounces	11 - 13	HI (max. power)	Follow package directions. Stir every 3 minutes. Use 4-cup glass measure.

COOKING/WARMING/DEFROSTING GUIDE — CONVENIENCE BREADS

Food	Amount	Power Control Setting	Time	Special Notes
Hamburger buns, hot dog rolls, frozen	1 lb.	50 (defrost)	3 - 4 minutes	Use original microproof container, paper plate, or towels. Place on microproof rack, turn over after 2 minutes.
Room temperature	1	HI (max. power)	10 - 15 seconds	
	2	HI (max. power)	15 - 20 seconds	
	4	HI (max. power)	20 - 25 seconds	
	6	HI (max. power)	25 - 30 seconds	
Doughnuts, sweet rolls, muffins	1	HI (max. power)	15 - 20 seconds	Place on paper plate or towel. Add 15 seconds if frozen.
	2	HI (max. power)	25 - 30 seconds	
	4	HI (max. power)	40 - 50 seconds	
	6	HI (max. power)	50 - 60 seconds	
Whole coffee-cake, frozen	10 - 13 oz.	HI (max. power)	2 - 2½ minutes	Place on paper plate or towel.
Room temperature	10 - 13 oz.	HI (max. power)	1¼ - 1¾ minutes	Place on paper plate or towel.
French bread, frozen	1 lb.	HI (max. power)	2 - 2¾ minutes	Place on paper plate or towel.
Room temperature	1 lb.	HI (max. power)	25 - 35 seconds	
English muffins, waffles, frozen	2	HI (max. power)	45 - 60 seconds	Place on paper towels. Toast in toaster after defrosting, if desired.
Corn bread mix	15 oz.	HI (max. power)	15 - 16 minutes	Use 9" round dish, paper-lined custard cups, or microproof muffin tray. Turn dish if rising unevenly. Let stand 5 minutes before serving.
Nut bread	6 muffins	HI (max. power)	3 - 4 minutes	Let stand 2 minutes before serving.
mix	15 - 17 oz.	HI (max. power)	20 minutes	Use 1½-quart bowl with glass in center. Let stand 5 minutes before serving.
Blueberry muffin mix	4	HI (max. power)	1 - 2 minutes	Use paper-lined custard cups or microproof muffin tray. Let stand 2 minutes before serving.
	6	HI (max. power)	3 - 4 minutes	
Bread, frozen	1 slice	50 (defrost)	15 - 20 seconds	Place on paper plate or towels. Let stand 5 minutes before serving.
	1 lb. loaf	50 (defrost)	2 - 3 minutes	In original plastic bag, remove twister. Let stand 5 minutes before serving.
Coffeecake mix	19 oz.	HI (max. power)	17 - 19 minutes	Use 9" round dish. Turn dish if rising unevenly. Let stand 5 minutes before serving.

Holiday Bread Ring _____ 10 to 12 servings

Total Cooking Time: 12 to 13 minutes

¾ cup milk
½ cup butter or margarine
2¼ to 3 cups all-purpose flour
¼ cup sugar
1 egg
1 package active dry
   yeast
1 teaspoon salt
1 teaspoon cardamom seeds
½ cup raisins
¼ cup chopped nuts
¼ cup chopped candied red
   cherries
1 tablespoon grated fresh
   orange peel
2 tablespoons sugar
1 teaspoon cinnamon
¼ cup sliced almonds

In 2-cup glass measure, combine milk and butter. Cook on HI (max. power) 2 minutes, or until warm (120°F if using the temperature probe). Stir to melt butter.

In large mixing bowl, combine 2 cups flour, sugar, egg, yeast, salt, cardamom, and warm milk mixture. Mix with electric mixer 3 to 4 minutes. Stir in raisins, chopped nuts, cherries, and orange peel. Stir in enough flour to form soft dough.

Generously grease 10-cup micro-proof bundt-type pan. Combine sugar and cinnamon. Sprinkle inside of prepared pan, shaking to coat all sides; use all mixture. Sprinkle almonds in bottom. Spoon batter into pan; spread evenly. Cover with plastic wrap. Fill a tall, thin glass with 1 cup water. Place pan and water in oven. Cook on 50 (defrost) 2 minutes. Let stand 1 hour in oven or out of draft.

When dough has doubled, remove plastic wrap and glass of water. Cook on HI (max. power) 8 to 9 minutes, or until bread springs back when lightly touched. Rotate dish, if bread is cooking unevenly. Let stand 10 minutes. Invert onto serving plate; cool before serving.

Pumpkin Cupcakes (page 150), Holiday Bread Ring →

Pumpkin Cupcakes _____ 12 servings

Total Cooking Time: 12 to 13 minutes

1 egg
½ cup firmly packed brown
   sugar
¼ cup sugar
6 tablespoons vegetable oil
½ cup canned or cooked
   mashed pumpkin
½ teaspoon vanilla
1 cup all-purpose flour
2 tablespoons milk
½ teaspoon cinnamon
½ teaspoon salt
¼ teaspoon baking powder
¼ teaspoon baking soda
⅛ teaspoon ginger
   Cream Cheese Frosting
      (page 154)

In mixing bowl, beat egg, sugars, and oil until smooth. Blend in pumpkin and vanilla. Add remaining ingredients, except frosting; stir until smooth. Line 6 cups in microproof cupcake pan or 6 glass custard cups with paper liners. Fill ½ full with batter. Cook on 50 (defrost) 6 to 6½ minutes, or until cupcakes test done, rotating cups if rising unevenly. Repeat with remaining batter. Cool and frost with Cream Cheese Frosting.

Pecan Rum Pie _____ 6 to 8 servings

Total Cooking Time: 11 to 12 minutes

¼ cup butter or margarine
1½ cups pecan halves
1 cup sugar
½ cup dark corn syrup
3 eggs, slightly beaten
1 teaspoon rum flavoring or
   vanilla extract
1 baked (9-inch) pie shell
   in microproof dish

Place butter in 2-quart glass bowl. Cook on HI (max. power) 1 minute, or until melted. Blend in nuts, sugar, corn syrup, eggs, and rum. Pour into pie shell. Cook on HI (max. power) 10 to 11 minutes, or until center is set. Cool to room temperature before serving.

Cheesecake and Raspberry Sauce _____ 6 to 8 servings

Total Cooking Time: 9½ to 13½ minutes

¾ cup graham cracker crumbs
¾ cup sugar, divided
3 tablespoons butter or margarine
2 tablespoons firmly packed brown sugar
1 teaspoon cinnamon
1 package (8 ounces) cream cheese, quartered
2 eggs
1 teaspoon vanilla
1 cup dairy sour cream
Raspberry Sauce (page 171)

Combine crumbs, 2 tablespoons of sugar, butter, brown sugar, and cinnamon in 8-inch round microproof cake dish. Cook on HI (max. power) 1½ to 2 minutes. Stir to combine. Press crumbs evenly over bottom and sides of cake dish.

Place cream cheese in small microproof bowl. Cook on 50 (defrost) 1 minute, or until softened. Gradually beat in ½ cup of sugar until dissolved. Add eggs and vanilla; mix well. Pour into prepared crust. Cook on HI (max. power) 6 to 8 minutes, or until nearly set in center, rotating dish if cake is cooking unevenly.

In small bowl, combine sour cream and remaining 2 tablespoons sugar; blend well. Spread carefully and evenly over filling. Cook on HI (max. power) 1½ to 2½ minutes, rotating after 1 minute. Edges should be set and center still soft. Cool to room temperature. Refrigerate at least 12 hours. Pass Raspberry Sauce with sliced cheesecake.

Cheesecake can be topped with any fruit in season, such as blueberries, strawberries, or peaches.

Chocolate Cherry Bundt Cake — 10 to 12 servings
Total Cooking Time: 20 minutes

1 tablespoon sugar
1 package (18½ ounces)
　　chocolate cake mix
　　with pudding
1 cup cherry pie filling
3 eggs
¾ cup water
¼ cup vegetable oil
1 teaspoon almond extract
　　White Cap Glaze (below)

Generously grease 12-cup microproof bundt-type pan; chill. Sprinkle with 1 tablespoon sugar; shake well to coat. Mix remaining ingredients, except glaze, following cake package directions. Pour carefully into prepared pan. Cook on 90 (bake) 20 minutes, or until cake tests done, rotating one-quarter turn at 5 minute intervals. Let stand 10 minutes before inverting onto serving plate to cool. Drizzle White Cap Glaze over cake. Let stand until glaze sets. Serve.

For an extra festive treat, top cake with additional cherries from remaining pie filling.

White Cap Glaze —————————————————— ½ cup
Total Cooking Time: 1 minute

1 package (3 ounces) cream
　　cheese
¾ cup confectioners' sugar
3 to 4 teaspoons milk

Remove foil from cream cheese. Place in 1-quart microproof bowl. Cook on 50 (defrost) 1 minute, or until softened. Beat in sugar and milk until smooth.

Chocolate Cherry Bundt Cake→

Raisin-Oatmeal Muffins _____ 18 servings
Total Cooking Time: 12 to 13½ minutes

1 cup all-purpose flour
⅔ cup quick-cooking oatmeal
¼ cup firmly packed brown
    sugar
1 teaspoon baking powder
½ teaspoon baking soda
½ teaspoon salt
1½ teaspoons cinnamon,
    divided
2 eggs
½ cup vegetable oil
½ cup buttermilk
½ cup raisins
2 tablespoons sugar

In small mixing bowl, combine flour, oatmeal, brown sugar, baking powder, baking soda, salt, and ½ teaspoon cinnamon. Add eggs, oil, buttermilk, and raisins. Stir until just moistened. Spoon batter into 6 paper-lined custard cups or microproof muffin pan, filling each about half full. Mix remaining cinnamon and sugar. Sprinkle top of each muffin with about ¼ teaspoon sugar-cinnamon mixture. Place 6 custard cups in a circle in oven. Cook on HI (max. power) 4 to 4½ minutes, rotating cups or pan if muffins are rising unevenly. Repeat with remaining batter. Serve warm.

Cream Cheese Frosting _____ 1½ cups
Total Cooking Time: 1 minute

1 package (3 ounces) cream
    cheese
2 tablespoons butter or
    margarine
2 cups confectioners sugar
½ teaspoon vanilla
1 to 2 teaspoons milk

In 1-quart microproof bowl, combine cream cheese and butter. Cook on HI (max. power) 1 minute, or until softened. Beat in sugar, vanilla, and enough milk for spreading consistency.

Butter Pecan Ice Cream Pie _____ 6 to 8 servings

Total Cooking Time: 7 to 8 minutes

6 tablespoons butter or
   margarine
¾ cup all-purpose flour
¾ cup finely ground pecans,
   divided
3 tablespoons firmly packed
   brown sugar
1 quart butter pecan
   ice cream

Place butter in 4-cup glass measure. Cook on HI (max. power) 1½ minutes, or until melted. Stir in flour, half of the pecans, and sugar; mix well. Press mixture firmly onto bottom and sides of 9-inch microproof pie plate. Cook on HI (max. power) 4½ minutes, rotating after 2 minutes. Cool to room temperature. Spoon ice cream into shell. (If ice cream is very firm, place carton on microproof plate. Cook on 50 (defrost) 1 to 2 minutes, or until softened.) Sprinkle remaining pecans over top. Freeze until firm.

Granola Crunch Cake _____ 12 servings

Total Cooking Time: 18 minutes

1 tablespoon sugar
1½ cups granola, divided
1 package (18½ ounces)
   yellow cake mix
1 package (3⅝ ounces)
   instant butterscotch
   pudding
3 eggs
¾ cup water
¼ cup vegetable oil

Generously grease 10-cup fluted microproof bundt-type pan; chill. Sprinkle inside with sugar; shake to coat all sides. Sprinkle ¼ cup of the granola into prepared pan.

In large mixing bowl, combine cake and pudding mixes, eggs, water, and oil. Mix according to cake package directions. Carefully pour three-fourths of the granola over batter in prepared pan. Sprinkle remaining granola over batter. Add remaining batter. Cook on 90 (bake) 18 minutes, or until cake tests done, rotating one-quarter turn every 5 minutes. Let stand 10 minutes. Invert onto serving plate. Cool before slicing.

Upside-Down Apple Cake ——————— 1 8-inch cake

Total Cooking Time: 19½ to 20½ minutes

1   cooking apple
¼   cup butter or margarine
⅓   cup honey
⅓   cup chopped nuts
¼   cup chopped maraschino
      cherries
1¼ cups all-purpose flour
¾   cup sugar
½   cup milk
⅓   cup shortening
1   egg
1½ teaspoons baking powder
1   teaspoon vanilla
½   teaspoon salt

Core unpeeled apple. Slice into ⅛-inch thick rings; cover and set aside.

Place butter in 9-inch microproof cake dish. Cook on HI (max. power) 1½ minutes, or until melted. Stir in honey. Add apple rings. Cook on HI (max. power) 4 minutes, turning apple rings after 2 minutes. Sprinkle with nuts and cherries; set aside.

In small mixing bowl, combine flour, sugar, milk, shortening, egg, baking powder, vanilla, and salt. Beat 3 minutes, scraping bowl once. Carefully spoon batter over apple rings in cake dish. Cook on 90 (bake) 14 to 15 minutes, or until cake tests done, rotating dish if cake is rising unevenly. Invert onto serving plate. Let cake stand in dish 3 to 4 minutes. Remove dish and let cake stand 10 minutes. Serve warm.

Pumpkin Walnut Bread ———————————— 1 loaf

Total Cooking Time: 17 to 19 minutes

2   tablespoons graham
      cracker crumbs
¾   cup firmly packed brown
      sugar
½   cup vegetable oil
2   eggs
2   tablespoons milk
1   cup canned or cooked
      mashed pumpkin
1   cup all-purpose flour
¾   cup chopped walnuts
⅛   teaspoon cinnamon
¾   teaspoon salt
½   teaspoon nutmeg
½   teaspoon baking powder
½   teaspoon baking soda

Grease bottom and sides of 8 × 4-inch microproof loaf dish. Sprinkle with graham cracker crumbs. Shake out excess; set aside.

In large mixing bowl, blend sugar and oil. Beat in eggs, milk, and pumpkin. Add remaining ingredients; mix well. Pour batter into prepared dish; spread evenly. Cook on HI (max. power) 17 to 19 minutes, or until bread tests done in center, rotating loaf during cooking time, if bread is rising unevenly. Let stand 10 minutes in dish. Remove from dish and let stand to cool completely. To develop flavor, wrap in foil and chill several hours before slicing. Serve with butter or cream cheese.

Maple Nut Ring _____ 6 servings

Total Cooking Time: 4½ to 5½ minutes

2 tablespoons butter or
   margarine
¼ cup firmly packed brown
   sugar
2 tablespoons chopped nuts
1 tablespoon maple syrup
1 teaspoon maple extract
1 can (10 ounces)
   refrigerator biscuits

Place butter in 8-inch microproof pie plate. Cook on HI (max. power) 1 minute, or until melted. Add sugar, nuts, syrup, and extract; blend well. Separate biscuit dough into 10 pieces. Arrange each piece in pie plate, slightly overlapping, to form a ring. Press biscuits gently together, leaving an opening in the center. Place glass custard cup in center. Cook on HI (max. power) 3½ to 4½ minutes, or until rolls spring back when lightly touched.

Remove custard cup. Invert onto serving plate. Syrup will run over bread ring. Remove pie plate. Let stand 3 minutes before serving.

Classic Coconut Cake _____ 10 to 12 servings

Total Cooking Time: 24 minutes

1 white cake mix
   (18½ ounces)
½ cup shredded coconut,
   finely chopped
1½ teaspoon grated lemon peel

Frosting

1 cup sugar
½ cup water
¼ teaspoon cream of tartar
   Dash of salt
2 egg whites
1 teaspoon vanilla
1 cup shredded coconut

Prepare cake mix according to package directions. Fold in ½ cup coconut and lemon peel. Pour half of batter into 9-inch microproof cake pan. Cook on 90 (bake) 8½ minutes, or until cake tests done. Rotate twice. Let stand 5 minutes on flat, heat resistant surface. Transfer to cool on wire rack. Repeat with remaining batter.

To prepare Frosting, combine sugar, water, cream of tartar, and salt in 2-cup glass measure. Cook on HI (max. power) 7 minutes. In a small mixing bowl, beat egg whites with an electric mixer until soft peaks form. Gradually add hot syrup mixture to egg whites, beating continuously. Continue beating 5 minutes, or until mixture is thick and fluffy. While beating, add vanilla. Frost cake and sprinkle with coconut on top and sides.

Brown & Serve Rolls _____ 12 rolls

Total Cooking Time: 24 to 29 minutes

1 loaf (1 pound) frozen
   bread dough

Place frozen dough on lightly greased 9-inch pie plate. Fill 1-cup glass measure with water. Cook on HI (max. power) 3 to 3½ minutes, or until water boils. Move water to rear of unit, cover dough with a damp cloth. Place in oven. Cook on 50 (defrost) 2½ minutes; turn loaf over. Cook on 50 (defrost) 2½ minutes. Form into twelve rolls or eighteen ¾-inch balls. Place three ¾-inch balls into each greased muffin cup. Set dough aside in a warm draft-free area until it doubles in size. When doubled, cook six at once on HI (max. power) 4 to 6 minutes, rotating dish twice. Repeat for remaining rolls. When rolls are done, the center should spring back when lightly touched. Refrigerate until ready to brown.

Before baking, rolls may be brushed with butter and coated with crushed dry onion flakes or buttered bread crumbs, poppy or sesame seeds. For an added touch before browning in the toaster oven or conventional oven, brush with beaten egg wash to give a professional bakery gloss.

Rice Pie Crust _____ One 9-inch pie shell

Total Cooking Time: 2 to 2½ minutes

1½ cups cooked rice
 1 egg, slightly beaten
⅓ cup shredded Cheddar
   cheese
 1 tablespoon parsley flakes

In mixing bowl, combine all ingredients; mix well. Press evenly over bottom and sides of 9-inch glass pie plate. Cook on HI (max. power) 2 to 2½ minutes, or until cheese is melted.

This crust is naturally low in calories. It can be used with many different fillings and is especially nice as the base for Onion Pie in Rice Crust (page 75).

Savory Cheese Bread _____ 2 loaves

Total Cooking Time: 16 to 18 minutes

1   cup milk
½   cup butter or margarine
2¾ cups all-purpose flour
2   tablespoons sugar
½   teaspoon salt
1   package (1 ounce) active
    dry yeast
1   egg
1   envelope onion soup mix,
    divided
1   cup shredded Cheddar
    cheese, divided

In 2-cup glass measure, combine milk and butter. Cook on HI (max. power) 2 minutes, or to 120°F on a microwave food thermometer.

In large mixing bowl, mix flour, sugar, salt, and yeast. Add milk mixture and egg. In small bowl, mix 2 tablespoons of soup mix and ¼ cup of cheese; set aside. Add remaining soup mix and cheese to batter.

Divide batter evenly between 2 well-greased 8×4×3-inch microproof loaf pans. Sprinkle with reserved onion-cheese mixture. Cover lightly. Let rise in warm place, free from draft, 1 to 1½ hours, or until double in volume. Cook 1 loaf at a time. Cook on HI (max. power) 7 to 8 minutes, or until bread springs back when lightly touched, sides recede from pan, and top is no longer moist. Turn out of pans and cool on wire rack.

Garlic Bread _____ 12 servings

Total Cooking Time: 1½ to 2 minutes

1   loaf (16 ounces) French,
    Italian, or sourdough
    bread
½   cup butter or margarine,
    softened
2   cloves garlic, minced or
    1 teaspoon garlic
    powder
½   cup grated Parmesan or
    Romano cheese
    Paprika

Cut loaf in 1-inch thick slices without cutting through bottom crust. In small bowl, blend butter and garlic. Spread on bread slices; then sprinkle with cheese and paprika. Place loaf on paper towel-lined microproof plate. Cook on HI (max. power) 1½ to 2 minutes, or until heated through.

Onion Herb Bread _____ 12 servings

Total Cooking Time: 1½ to 2 minutes

1 loaf (16 ounces) French,
   Italian, or sourdough
   bread
½ cup butter or margarine,
   softened
1 tablespoon instant onion
   flakes
1 tablespoon snipped parsley
½ teaspoon dillweed
¼ teaspoon onion salt
   Paprika

Cut loaf in 1-inch thick slices without cutting through bottom crust. In small bowl, blend remaining ingredients, except paprika. Spread on bread slices. Sprinkle with paprika. Place loaf on paper towel-lined microproof plate. Cook on HI (max. power) 1½ to 2 minutes, or until heated through.

SPECIAL TREATS

Carefully select the microproof cookware for bar cookies (left). If you don't have a microproof candy thermometer, check with conventional, outside the oven (above).

If you're like many cooks, candy has been one of those items yet to achieve homemade status with you. That's about to change and you'll never regret it! The fuss and mess of double boilers has been eliminated by the microwave oven. It's truly so easy that you'll soon laugh to yourself as friends are amazed by your talent.

You'll also soon be churning out an array of bar cookies that will have a line of neighborhood kids at your kitchen door. Raisin-Nut Bars (page 167) and Lemon Bars (page 168) were the favorites of the test kitchen but be sure to try your own recipes, too, and others here.

Fruit specialties and sauces are also excellent and easier than — well, everything *is* easy in the microwave, isn't it?

We hope you've enjoyed this book and, more importantly, are convinced that the world of microwave cooking is a special treat of its own. Good fortune and good cooking to you!

Converting Your Recipes

To make candy, simply find a similar recipe here. You'll be trying all those recipes you've been longing to do. For other desserts, consult these tips as well as similar recipes:

☐ You can enhance your light batter cookies and cakes with cinnamon, nutmeg, brown sugar, coffee, nuts, toppings, frostings, glazes, food coloring, etc.

☐ Small drop cookies and slice 'n bake cookies don't do as well as the larger bar cookies. Drop cookies must be cooked in small batches; they tend to cook unevenly, and need to be removed individually from the oven when finished.

☐ A serviceable cookie sheet can be made by covering cardboard with waxed paper.

☐ For even cooking, select fruit of uniform size to be cooked whole, as in baked apples, or to be cooked in pieces, as in apple pie.

☐ Stirring sauces quickly two or three times during cooking is sufficient to ensure even cooking. Too many stirrings may slow cooking.

COOKING/DEFROSTING GUIDE — CONVENIENCE DESSERTS

Food	Amount	Power Control Setting	Time	Special Notes
Brownies, other bars, frozen	12 - 13 oz.	50 (defrost)	2 - 3 minutes	In original ¾" foil tray, lid removed. Let stand 5 minutes.
Cookies, frozen	6	50 (defrost)	50 - 60 seconds	Place on paper plate or towels.
Pineapple upside-down cake mix	21½ oz.	75 (simmer) HI (max. power)	10 - 12 minutes	Use 9" round glass dish. Remove enough batter for 2 cupcakes, bake separately. Rotate if rising unevenly.
Cupcakes or crumb cakes, frozen	1 or 2	50 (defrost)	½ - 1 minute	Place on shallow plate.
Cheesecake, frozen	17 - 19 oz.	50 (defrost)	3 - 4 minutes	Remove from foil pan to plate. Let stand 1 minute.
Pound cake, frozen	10¾ oz.	50 (defrost)	2 minutes	Remove from foil pan to plate. Rotate once. Let stand 5 minutes.
Cake, frozen 2- or 3-layer	17 oz.	50 (defrost)	2 - 3 minutes	Remove from foil pan to plate. Watch carefully, frosting melts fast. Let stand 5 minutes.
Custard pie, frozen	9" pie	HI (max. power)	5 - 6 minutes	Remove from foil pan to plate. Center should be nearly set.
Fruit pie, frozen, unbaked, 2 crusts	9" pie	HI (max. power)	17 - 20 minutes	On glass pie plate. Brown, if desired, in preheated 425° conventional oven 8 - 10 minutes.
Frozen fruit	10 oz.	HI (max. power)	6½ - 7½ minutes	On microproof plate. Slit pouch. Flex halfway through cooking time to mix.
	16 oz.	HI (max. power)	5 - 6 minutes	Remove from bag. Place in glass casserole, cover. Stir halfway through cooking time.
Cake mix	18½ oz.	75 (simmer) HI (max. power)	20 - 21 minutes	Follow package directions. 10-cup bundt-type pan. Rotate every 5 minutes.

Chocolate Fudge _____ 3 pounds

Total Cooking Time: 11 to 14 minutes

3 cups sugar
½ cup butter or margarine
1 can (5⅓ ounces)
  evaporated milk
2 cups (12 ounces) semisweet
  chocolate pieces
1 jar (7 ounces) marshmallow
  creme
1 cup chopped nuts
1 teaspoon vanilla

Lightly butter a 13×9-inch baking pan. Combine sugar, butter, and milk in 2-quart glass bowl. Cook on HI (max. power) 11 to 14 minutes, or until a small amount dropped in cold water forms a soft ball (234°F on microproof candy thermometer). Stir in chocolate pieces and marshmallow creme until mixture is thoroughly blended. Stir in nuts and vanilla. Pour into prepared pan. Refrigerate until firm. Cut into squares.

If using a conventional thermometer, do not leave in oven during cooking.

Cinnamon-Sugar Nuts _____ 2 cups

Total Cooking Time: 5 to 6 minutes

1 large egg white (about
  2 tablespoons)
2 cups (8 ounces) pecan
  halves
¼ cup firmly packed brown
  sugar
1 teaspoon cinnamon

Combine egg white and pecans in small bowl; mix until pecans are moistened. In another small bowl, combine brown sugar and cinnamon; mix well. Add to nuts; mix until coated. Pour into greased 9-inch microproof pie plate. Cook on HI (max. power) 5 to 6 minutes, or until coating is no longer glossy, stirring twice during cooking time. Let stand until cool. Store in airtight container.

Fairy Food _____ 1 pound
Total Cooking Time: 16 to 18½ minutes

1 cup sugar
1 cup dark corn syrup
1 tablespoon vinegar
1 tablespoon baking soda
1 pound semisweet dipping
    chocolate
1 tablespoon shortening

Line 8-inch square baking dish with aluminum foil; butter generously; set aside.

In 2-quart glass bowl, combine sugar, corn syrup, and vinegar. Cook on HI (max. power) 5 minutes, stirring several times during cooking time. Continue to cook on HI (max. power) 8 to 10 minutes, or until mixture is thickened and microproof candy thermometer registers 300°F (or a small amount dropped in cold water separates into hard, brittle threads). Quickly stir in baking soda; blend well. Pour into prepared dish. Spread evenly with spoon or tip baking dish to cover bottom evenly. Let stand 1 hour, or until firm. Break hardened mixture into pieces; set aside.

Break up chocolate and place in 2-quart glass measure. Add shortening. Cook on HI (max. power) 3 to 3½ minutes, or until melted, stirring once during cooking. Dip hardened pieces in chocolate, covering completely. Place on waxed paper to cool. Store in refrigerator in an airtight container.

Chocolate Almond Bark _____ 1½ pounds
Total Cooking Time: 7½ to 8½ minutes

1 cup blanched whole
    almonds
1 teaspoon butter or
    margarine
1 pound semisweet or milk
    chocolate

Combine almonds and butter in 9-inch glass pie plate. Cook on HI (max. power) 4½ to 5 minutes, or until almonds are golden, stirring twice during cooking time; set aside. Place chocolate in 2-quart glass bowl. Cook on HI (max. power) 3 to 3½ minutes, or until melted. Stir in almonds. Pour onto waxed paper-lined baking sheet. Spread to desired thickness. Refrigerate until firm. Break into pieces to serve. Store in cool place.

Dry-Roasted Peanut Brittle ———— about 1 pound

Total Cooking Time: 11 to 12 minutes

1 cup sugar
½ cup light corn syrup
1¾ cups dry-roasted unsalted peanuts
1 tablespoon butter or margarine
1 teaspoon vanilla
1 teaspoon baking soda

Generously grease baking sheet. In 2-quart microproof bowl, combine sugar and corn syrup. Cook on HI (max. power) 6 minutes. Stir in peanuts with wooden spoon. Cook on HI (max. power) 5 to 6 minutes, or until mixture reaches 300°F on microproof candy thermometer (or a small amount separates into hard, brittle threads when dropped in cold water). Stir in butter and vanilla. Blend in baking soda; stir until mixture is light and foamy. Pour onto prepared sheet; spread quickly. As candy cools, stretch into thin sheet using buttered hands. Cool completely. Break into pieces and store in an airtight container.

Pumpkin Mousse ———— 8 servings

Total Cooking Time: 5 to 5½ minutes

½ cup evaporated milk
1 envelope unflavored gelatin
1 cup pumpkin pie filling
¼ cup firmly packed brown sugar
2 eggs, separated
½ teaspoon cinnamon
2 tablespoons sugar
1½ cups sweetened whipped cream or thawed frozen whipped topping, divided
Nutmeg

Combine milk and gelatin in 1-quart microproof bowl; let stand to soften gelatin. Stir in pumpkin pie filling, brown sugar, egg yolks, and cinnamon; beat until smooth. Cook on HI (max. power) 5 to 5½ minutes, or until mixture begins to boil, stirring every 2 minutes. Refrigerate until thickened.

In small mixing bowl, beat egg whites until frothy. Gradually beat in 2 tablespoons sugar until stiff peaks form. Fold 1 cup of whipped topping into cooled pumpkin mixture. Gently fold in egg whites. Spoon into 8 sherbet glasses. Refrigerate until chilled. Top with remaining whipped topping. Sprinkle with nutmeg.

Poached Pears _____ 8 servings

Total Cooking Time: 21 minutes

4 cups water, divided
3 tablespoons lemon juice
4 firm, ripe pears (6 to 8
    ounces each)
1 cup dry red wine
⅓ cup sugar
1 cinnamon stick
  Lemon peel strip

In mixing bowl, combine 3 cups of water and lemon juice. Peel pears; cut in half lengthwise; core. Place pears in lemon-water.

In 2-quart microproof casserole, combine remaining water, wine, sugar, cinnamon, and lemon peel. Cook on HI (max. power) 7 minutes. Remove pears from water with slotted spoon; add to hot wine mixture. Turn pear halves to coat completely. Cover with waxed paper. Cook on HI (max. power) 14 minutes, or until pears are tender, turning pears twice during cooking time. Let stand, in syrup, until cool. Serve in sherbet dishes.

Cherries Jubilee _____ 6 to 8 servings

Total Cooking Time: 9 minutes

1 can (1 pound, 14 ounces)
    pitted bing cherries,
    ¼ cup juice reserved
1 jar (10 ounces) currant
    jelly
1 tablespoon lemon juice
1½ teaspoons cornstarch
1 teaspoon grated orange
    rind
¼ cup brandy

Combine reserved cherry juice, jelly, lemon juice, cornstarch, and orange rind in 2-quart glass measure or microproof bowl, stirring to dissolve cornstarch. Cook on HI (max. power) 4½ minutes, or until thickened, stirring once during cooking time. Add cherries. Cook on HI (max. power) 3½ minutes. Pour brandy into 1-cup glass measure. Cook on 50 (defrost) 1 minute. Ignite brandy and pour over cherry mixture. Serve, flaming, over vanilla ice cream or angel food cake.

If serving from a chafing dish, transfer cooked cherry mixture to dish before heating brandy. If serving over ice cream, spoon ice cream into serving dishes and place in freezer before sauce is cooked.

Marshmallow Crisp ———————— 36 bars
Total Cooking Time: 4 to 5 minutes

¼ cup butter or margarine
5 cups miniature (or 40 large) marshmallows
5 cups crispy rice cereal
1 cup chopped nuts

Lightly grease 12×7×2-inch baking dish; set aside. Place butter in 3-quart microproof casserole. Cook on HI (max. power) 1 to 1½ minutes, or until melted. Add marshmallows. Cover. Cook on HI (max. power) 3 to 3½ minutes, or until soft, stirring once during cooking time. Stir to combine marshmallows and butter. Add cereal and nuts; stir until thoroughly coated. Press warm mixture into prepared dish. Let stand until cool. Cut into bars.

Raisin-Nut Bars ———————— 18 to 20 bars
Total Cooking Time: 12½ to 15½ minutes

1 cup raisins, chopped
½ cup apple juice
2 tablespoons sugar
1 teaspoon all-purpose flour
½ cup chopped nuts, divided
½ cup butter or margarine, room temperature
½ cup firmly packed brown sugar
1 teaspoon vanilla
1 teaspoon baking powder
¾ cup all-purpose flour
1½ cups quick-cooking oats

Combine raisins, apple juice, sugar, and the 1 teaspoon flour in 4-cup glass measure. Cover with plastic wrap. Cook on HI (max. power) 4 to 5 minutes, or until thickened, stirring once during cooking time. Stir in ¼ cup of nuts; set aside.

In mixing bowl, cream butter, brown sugar, and vanilla. Mix baking powder with ¾ cup flour; add to creamed mixture. Stir in oats and remaining nuts. Press half of the flour mixture into 8-inch round microproof baking dish. Cook on HI (max. power) 2½ to 3½ minutes, or until surface is no longer moist. Spread raisin mixture on top. Spoon remaining flour mixture over raisin filling; press lightly. Cook on HI (max. power) 6 to 7 minutes, or until no longer moist on top. Let stand in pan on heat-resistant counter top or breadboard until cool. Cut into squares.

Lemon Bars _____ 16 bars

Total Cooking Time: 11 to 13 minutes

1 cup all-purpose flour
½ cup butter or margarine, room temperature
⅓ cup confectioners sugar
2 eggs
1 cup sugar
2 tablespoons flour
2 tablespoons lemon juice
1 teaspoon grated lemon rind
½ teaspoon baking powder
Confectioners sugar

Mix flour, butter, and ⅓ cup confectioners sugar until crumbly. Press into bottom of 8-inch square microproof pan. Cook on HI (max. power) 5 minutes. Combine remaining ingredients, except last addition of confectioners sugar; beat with electric mixer until smooth. Pour over baked crust. Cook on HI (max. power) 6 to 8 minutes, or until center tests done, rotating dish if bars are rising unevenly. Let stand, covered with waxed paper, 4 minutes. Remove waxed paper, cool, and cut into bars. Sprinkle with confectioners sugar.

Granola Nut Drops _____ 36 servings

Total Cooking Time: 2½ to 3½ minutes

1 package (6 ounces) semi-sweet chocolate pieces
1 tablespoon peanut butter
1½ cups granola with coconut and nuts
½ cup wheat flakes cereal
½ cup chopped dates
½ cup raisins

Combine chocolate and peanut butter in 2-quart glass bowl. Cook on HI (max. power) 2½ to 3½ minutes, or until chocolate is melted. Stir until smooth. Add remaining ingredients and stir until thoroughly coated. Drop by teaspoonfuls onto waxed paper. Chill until firm.

Lemon Bars, Dry-Roasted Peanut Brittle (page 165)→

Chewy Coconut Bars _____ 18 to 20 bars
Total Cooking Time: 8½ to 9½ minutes

½ cup butter or margarine
2 eggs
¾ cup firmly packed brown
  sugar
½ cup all-purpose flour
1 teaspoon baking powder
1 teaspoon vanilla
1 cup chopped nuts
1 cup flaked coconut
  Confectioners sugar

Place butter in 1-cup glass measure. Cook on HI (max. power) 1½ minutes, or until melted; set aside. In mixing bowl, beat eggs until light and fluffy. Add brown sugar, flour, baking powder, vanilla, and melted butter; blend thoroughly. Stir in nuts and coconut. Pour into 8-inch square microproof baking dish. Cook on HI (max. power) 7 to 8 minutes, rotating dish once during cooking time. Mixture will be moist, but will firm as it cools. Let stand on heat-resistant counter top or breadboard until cool. Sprinkle with confectioners sugar. Cut into squares.

Peanut Chocolate Sauce _____ 1 cup
Total Cooking Time: 4 minutes

1 square (1 ounce) unsweetened
  baking chocolate
¼ cup milk
1 cup sugar
2 tablespoons butter or
  margarine
¼ teaspoon vanilla
1 cup chopped salted
  peanuts

In 4-cup glass measure, combine chocolate and milk. Cook on HI (max. power) 2 minutes, or until chocolate is melted; stir. Stir in sugar. Cook on HI (max. power) 2 minutes, or until mixture boils. Stir in butter and vanilla, until butter is melted. Stir in nuts. Serve warm or cold over ice cream or cake.

Applesauce _____ 4 servings
Total Cooking Time: 5 to 7 minutes

4 tart cooking apples,
  cored and sliced
  (peeled, if desired)
1 tablespoon sugar
1 teaspoon cinnamon

Arrange apple slices in 1½-quart microproof baking dish. Mix sugar and cinnamon; sprinkle over apples. Cover. Cook on HI (max. power) 5 to 7 minutes. Transfer to blender or food processor; blend to desired consistency.

Caramel Sauce _____ 1 cup

Total Cooking Time: 3½ to 4½ minutes

½ pound (28) vanilla
   caramels
⅓ cup water
¼ cup chopped nuts

In 4-cup glass measure, combine caramels and water. Cook on HI (max. power) 3½ to 4½ minutes, or until melted. Stir until smooth. Stir in nuts. Serve over ice cream, cake, baked apples, or fruit cobblers.

Raspberry Sauce _____ ¾ cup

Total Cooking Time: 9 to 9½ minutes

1 package (10 ounces)
   frozen raspberries
2 teaspoons cornstarch
1 teaspoon lemon juice

Place frozen berries in 4-cup glass measure. Cook on 50 (defrost) 3 to 3½ minutes, or until thawed. Drain juice, reserve. Combine cornstarch with 1 tablespoon of raspberry juice; mix to make a paste. Stir in remaining raspberry juice. Stir in berries. Cook on HI (max. power) 6 minutes, stirring every 1 minute. Stir in lemon juice. Chill before serving. Serve over ice cream, cheesecake, pudding, or butter cake.

Cranberry Sauce _____ 2 cups

Total Cooking Time: 8 to 9 minutes

1 package (12 ounces)
   fresh cranberries
   (about 3 cups)
½ cup sugar
⅓ cup water
⅛ teaspoon almond extract

Combine all ingredients, except almond extract, in 2-quart microproof bowl. Cover with plastic wrap. Cook on HI (max. power) 8 to 9 minutes, or until berries pop. Stir in almond extract. Let stand until cool. Cover and refrigerate until ready to serve.

INDEX

(Recipe page appears in dark type when two or more pages are cited.)

174